FRED ASTAIRE

A WONDERFUL LIFE

Other Books by Bill Adler

The Kennedy Wit
The Cosby Wit
Sinatra: The Man and the Myth
Elizabeth Taylor: Triumph and Tragedy
Ronnie and Nancy: A Very Special Love Story

FRED ASTAIRE
A WONDERFUL LIFE

A BIOGRAPHY BY BILL ADLER

Carroll & Graf Publishers, Inc.
New York

First Carroll & Graf edition 1987

Carroll & Graf Publishers, Inc.
260 Fifth Avenue
New York, NY 10001

Photographs by courtesy of AP/WIDE WORLD PHOTOS.

Cover photo by courtesy of The Kobal Collection.

Library of Congress Cataloging in Publication Data

Adler, Bill.
  Fred Astaire: a wonderful life.

  Bibliography: p.
  1. Astaire, Fred. 2. Dancers—United States—
Biography. 3. Actors—United States—Biography.
I. Title.
GV1785. A83A64 1987   793.3′2′0924 [B]   87-25019

ISBN: 0-88184-376-8

Manufactured in the United States of America

Contents

Part One
Moanin' Minnie (1899–33)

Part Two
The Austerlitz-McMath Connection (1933–39)

Part Three
The Renaissance Man (1939–87)

PART ONE

Moanin's Minnie (1899–33)

Chapter One

Cake Walk

He was born May 10, 1899, in Omaha, Nebraska, the second child and only son of a brewer and a housewife—their names Frederick E. Austerlitz and Ann Gelius Austerlitz. The new baby had an older sister named Adele, born eighteen months ahead of him.

Although the new son was named Frederick like his father, he was never officially "Frederick Austerlitz, Jr." because his name was changed at an early age to Astaire by his entertainment-oriented mother, who knew "Austerlitz" would never fit a theater marquee; besides, as her son once said, it would only get him mixed up with a famous European battleground.

His father had been born in Austria and was early on engaged in the beer trade. His real reason for emigrating from Vienna was never really clarified to his son's complete satisfaction, but there seemed to be some trouble between him and his older brother, Ernest.

According to the vague outlines of the story, Ernest was an officer in the Austrian army; Frederick, a junior officer. When Frederick once failed to salute his brother in a public street, Ernest took great offense and had Frederick thrown in the stockade for disobedience. As soon after that as he could decently leave the military service, the story went, Frederick immediately set sail for America.

Frederick did not particularly like New York City and immediately moved on westward until he had quite isolated himself in the middle of the vast country of his choice. In Omaha he found a job that suited him and his ambition and became a salesman for the Storz Brewing Company. That, of course, was a long time before Prohibition put an end to drinking—for a time—in the bustling new country. The émigré, a somewhat dashing young man, liked the business and soon prospered in it.

In Omaha the young Austrian met and fell in love with a teenage beauty named Ann Gelius. Ann was ten years younger than Frederick, but he was a person who could sweep a young woman off her feet—and he did. Somewhere along the line he had picked up the art of playing the piano, and Ann was impressed. For a long time she had dreamed of escaping from Omaha into the great world of entertainment—or, as it was called at that time, "show business."

Adele was Ann's firstborn, and almost immediately the Omaha shut-in decided that indeed she might be able to get out of Nebraska through her daughter and her daughter's talent. For Adele quite soon proved that she was an instinctive dancer, singer, and performer. From her first months, she was "on" whenever her father played tunes on the piano.

When young Frederick arrived, he soon picked up the ability to move about the way his sister did, even though he refused to go to dancing school when he was old enough to, in spite of Adele's success there. By now even Frederick, Sr., was impressed with Adele's abilities on the dance floor. At the age of four she began taking lessons at a school in Omaha called Chambers' Dancing Academy, located on West Farnum Street.

Occasionally when Ann went down to pick up Adele after her lesson, she would take young Frederick with her. A family story has it that one day when the young boy was sitting around waiting for his sister to finish, he saw a pair of ballet slippers on the floor and slipped into them. Being an instinctive mime, he tried to imitate the other girls by standing on his toes—and he did! "I am not certain that I recall the incident," Fred Astaire wrote sternly in his autobiography years later.

Nevertheless, Adele was pretty good at her dancing. She began to score at local school affairs and church entertainments. Being a year and half older than her brother, she had begun school and was appearing whenever she could in school shows.

"Mrs. Austerlitz always dreamed of escaping from Omaha through her children," said one family friend of those early years, putting into words Anne's personal obsession and demonstrating that in Omaha circles her dreams of fame and fortune were familiar.

To the average 1980s American, "escaping" from the boondocks is certainly nothing new, but the method devised by Ann Austerlitz is strange to us. How could she do it by getting her kids jobs in show business?

The answer is of course that turn-of-the-century America was quite a different place from 1980s America. There was no television. There was no cinema. There was no radio. Even transportation was not fully mechanized. There were no airplanes, no rapid transit, no instantaneous communication.

Yet there was a great deal of hustle and bustle in the rapidly growing country. The vitality and the optimism of the early 1900s were phenomena that gradually died out during the two world wars that followed and the Depression that separated them. After the cynicism and breakdown of tradition in the 1960s, that optimism and vitality never fully returned.

Ingrained in the American spirit at that time was the idea that if you worked hard you would succeed. Moreover, one could be whatever one wanted to be in this new country, which was not class-conscious and stratified the way most European countries were.

Anyone born in America could be president. Likewise, anyone born in the country could be a millionaire, as well. There were many ways to become rich then, as there are now. Although there was no television, no motion pictures, and no radio, there was entertainment galore. No one, even in as remote a spot as Omaha, was prevented from seeing great actors and actresses. They arrived in town for short stage appearances and then moved on.

In addition to the "higher theatrical arts"—opera and the legitimate stage—there was vaudeville and burlesque. Vaudeville was the most popular type of theater. Sometimes as many as twenty acts would be crammed into a program for the theatergoer to watch.

Vaudeville was also a great consumer of material. But more than that, it was a stage that newcomers could use to learn the trade of acting, singing, dancing, or whatever. There were dramatic acts, there were comic acts, there were musical acts in which groups sang popular songs. Among the many types of acts in a show, there was one usually devoted to kids: young boys and girls in groups, in pairs, or alone.

But vaudeville was run from New York City. It was where the acts were booked. For a parent to start his child or children on a career in show business—and why not, with the possibilities of making good money quite real in spite of the precarious life?—one had to be in New York, where the action was.

Although "brother and sister" seemed quite a tame pairing off, there were dozens of famous brother-and-sister acts during the years of vaudeville, and about these Ann Austerlitz read avidly. She read about the Cansinos (Elisa, Eduardo, Angel, and José). Eduardo Cansino was to become the father of a dancing daughter who would go on to star in Hollywood and dance in two Fred Astaire motion pictures—under her stage name, Rita Hayworth. She read about Vilma and Buddy Ebsen. Buddy went to Hollywood later to play Huck Finn to Jackie Coogan's Tom Sawyer, do some dancing, and eventually wow millions in the television sitcom *The Beverly Hillbillies* and reprise that hit with a detective series called *Barnaby Jones*.

But all that was far in the future. Ann Austerlitz knew what she was about when she decided to become a "backstage mother," in the jargon of the day, and get her kids out of Omaha.

Her dream—although when it came it was more in the form of a nightmare—materialized in 1904 when quite suddenly Frederick Austerlitz, Sr., was out of a job at the brewery. At that point Adele was six, and Fred was four and a half. The family held a quick but solemn meeting, and it was decided that it was now or never for that foray into the big time.

"Adele is a born dancer," Ann said.

Her husband nodded. "And maybe Fred will come around to it someday, too."

"Why not give them a chance to develop their talents?" Ann reasoned hopefully.

Young Fred had little to say about it. He had aspirations of a sort at that time, too; he wanted to become a baseball star. Dancing was strictly for girls. But if he *had* to do it . . .

Later, Fred Astaire looked back on those years with amusement. "There was a time . . . when I used to think of [Adele] with contempt. She couldn't play ball, or chin herself, or whistle through her teeth. She couldn't even spit! I used to pray at night for God to turn her into a brother."

Adele must have been doing the same thing as he was, praying for God to turn her brother into a sister. She even tied a silk ribbon on his hair to make her prayers come true. Instead of thanking her, Fred poked her in the eye.

The train ride from Omaha to New York took up two and a half days. That was exciting stuff for Fred. Adele and he ran up and down the aisles and made life miserable for the passengers and for their mother. But she soon put her foot down, and the children remained anchored for the time being.

Staying temporarily at the Herald Square Hotel, the would-be backstage mother and her two charges soon arrived at Claude Alvienne's Dancing School, where Fred and Adele were both enrolled. Ann had found the name of the school in the *New York Clipper*, a theatrical trade paper that Frederick Austerlitz subscribed to.

About this time Ann was conferring by mail with Frederick, Sr., back in Omaha. The decision was made for a name change. Austerlitz would become "Astaire," presumably more easily remembered not because it was a common name but because it was an interesting one. A stair was a step up, and that was going to be the way it would be. One step at a time, on up to the top!

At Alvienne's, work was going ahead for the two young dancers. Although dancing was indeed the *main* point of these kiddie acts, there was also the need for the spoken word and the sung word. And so the Alviennes taught dramatic reading as well as

10

dancing. Claude was a fatherly man, very "kind," as Fred remembered him. His wife, who had been known on the stage as "La Neva," a star toe dancer in the style of the time, helped out with the teaching.

Meanwhile, Ann was making daily calls at some of the seediest and raunchiest offices in New York City, trying to find out if there was an agent who would take on her two children to help them break into the rough-and-tough business of entertainment.

At this point it became evident that it was Adele who had the talent and Fred who had the durability. "I only started to dance in 1906 because my sister Adele did. I literally followed in her footsteps. I just went along for the ride." So said Fred Astaire many years later, looking back on those early and terrifying years.

The competition between Fred and Adele increased in intensity at this point. Fred said:

When we had the first contest at dancing school, Adele put in some crazy little jiggers that we hadn't prepared at all. I was all primed for murder—until the judges gave us the first prize, with special mention for Adele, and then it began to dawn on me that she had *her* way of getting results and I had mine. Gradually that idea sank in, until I understood that we got along together best if we admitted that we were entirely separate people.

Alvienne gave his charges exposure by presenting an occasional school recital. These were usually dance programs, but they sometimes included dramatic readings in order to give the backstage mothers the idea that they were getting something for their money.

The newly named "Astaires" were soon cast to star in a dramatic episode out of Edmond Rostand's *Cyrano de Bergerac*. After Ann tried to explain what the story was to Fred, he made the absolutely soul-destroying discovery that *he* was scheduled to do a love scene. More than that, Adele—who towered over him now at the age of seven to his five and a half—would be the male Cyrano, and he would be the female Roxane.

Roxane had long blond hair; that meant Fred would be decked out in a blond wig. It was his first encounter with a hairpiece. Later on, in his maturity, he would play before cameras in hairpieces for years and years because of a genetic heritage that had doomed him to early baldness. In fact, during a dramatic moment in 1946, after forty-one continuous years in show business, he decided to call it quits after finishing his last scene in a motion picture entitled *Blue Skies*.

When the director yelled "cut," he carefully removed his toupee, stared at it for a moment, and then, in full view of the entire cast and crew, slammed it down on the floor and jumped on it with a mixture of venom and glee.

"Never, never, never!" he shouted, "never will I have to wear that blasted rug again!"

And here it was, a kind of warning sign, back in 1905: a hairpiece that tickled the back of his neck—a harbinger for the years to come. Besides that, he was annoyed at the satin dress that kept getting in the way of his footwork, tripping him up.

Anyway, Adele wore the swashbuckler's rig as they played the balcony scene, waving her sword and doing all she was called on to do as Cyrano. It was a seventeen-minute recital of the lines from Rostand's dramatization of the French poet-philosopher-writer's love life.

It was deemed a success.

This was enough to inspire Claude Alvienne to dream up a special act for the Astaire siblings—once, of course, he had established the fact that Ann Austerlitz was willing to pay for the rather elaborate and complex "props" necessary for the idea he had in mind.

These props were two huge replicas in giant size of wedding cakes. They were built so that they could be danced on and were about six feet in diameter and at least two feet high off the stage floor. Of course, they had plywood tops that would support the weight of the two children.

In addition to that, these two wedding "cakes" were gimmicked up with electrically controlled bells and colored lights. The idea was for the two performers to "play" the drums with their hands and feet, ringing a bell at will and automatically turning on a bright light at the same time. In effect, they "made" their own music by "playing" the bells as they danced, beating out the tune of a current song called "Dreamland Waltz" with their toes.

So much for the elaborate "props." The costumes were something else again. To tie in with the wedding motif, Fred—playing the groom—was to wear full evening dress, complete with top hat and tails. Adele was all dressed in white satin as a bride.

But these costumes were only come-ons. Fred and Adele returned in different costumes for the second part of the act: Fred dressed up as a lobster; Adele, as a glass of champagne.

If Fred's hairpiece in the Cyrano act was a harbinger of future events, his costume as the groom in the wedding-cake act was a harbinger of something even more crucial; he would always be known as the dancer who wore top hat, white tie, and tails.

He was later to write: "The evil idea [of dressing up in formal clothes] was planted way back there."

They tried out the act at one of the school recitals. It started out with the two of them mounting the wedding cakes and dancing on their toes for a few passes, then knocking out the "Dreamland

Waltz" as they moved about. After winding up the duet, they ran off, with the cakes lighting up brightly almost as if by magic once they were gone.

Adele then returned for a solo dance in her bride's costume. Then Fred came out and did a solo in his formal outfit—a buck and wing on his toes. Quickly he left, made a rapid change, and reappeared as the lobster. Adele reappeared as the champagne glass.

The two of them did one of those goofy, eccentric dance duets and played a number of tunes on the electrically operated bells. The act ran a good twelve minutes, and it seemed to please the audiences.

Talk about cutesy-pie stuff! But that was the order of the day. The cuter the better, it was thought. And for kids the age the Astaires were, it was even more true than for more mature performers. Whatever it was, no one was looking back to criticize something that had gone over. The next step was to mount the act somewhere in the professional world.

Success couldn't be far off! Adele decided. Fred wasn't so sure. He had a way of always wondering what was going to work and what wasn't. It was at that period, when Fred began to see the darker side of everything, that Adele began to tease him, calling him "Moanin' Minnie." She always saw the bright side. He called her "Funny Face."

Largely on the strength of their success in the act at the school recital, the Astaires were hired to perform at a showplace in Keyport, New Jersey. They were billed, as Claude Alvienne had determined it, as "Juvenile Artists Presenting an Electric Musical Toe-Dancing Novelty." The word "electric" was of course used to describe the electric lights; electricity was still a novelty in certain parts of the country.

Their actual debut took place in 1907. Keyport, New Jersey, was what was then known as a "tryout" theater. Audiences at these affairs were very blasé and tough on the new acts they were regularly seeing. The women, who always seemed to sit in the front rows with dark scowls on their faces, were called "mothers who ate their young."

Whatever the Astaires had on that opening night was in their favor. "I think on the whole we did pretty well," Fred later wrote in his autobiography. He was much too modest. The two of them *wowed* the hard-eyed audience.

The Keyport newspaper wrote: "The Astaires are the greatest child act in vaudeville."

They were pros now.

They got fifty dollars a week for that first engagement.

Chapter Two

School Days

With the successful launching of the "Juvenile Artists Presenting an Electric Musical Toe-Dancing Novelty"—in other words, the Astaire siblings—a new element was added to the combination. Frederick Austerlitz, Sr., had up to this point more or less remained in the background in Omaha, taking sales jobs here and there and sending money to the struggling trio in New York.

Now it was obvious that both his and Ann's hopes about their youngsters were being realized. And so the senior Austerlitz hopped the train and arrived in New York to lend more than financial support to the newly established show-biz "act."

A personable, charming, and affable man, Frederick, Sr., was a born salesman. He now applied his talents to show-business problems, about which he knew little but intended to learn much. It was his aim to sell this combination to the New York bookers who called the turns in vaudeville.

Austerlitz was a fast read. In almost no time he had mastered the structure of the complex booking system then in operation in the Big Apple and had begun to ingratiate himself with many of the top theatrical agents, big-time and small-time producers, and key figures in the tangled jungle of the booking offices. Quite soon he was on speaking terms with many of the top guns of the industry.

At the same time he took on a job with Claude Alvienne to slick up the "Juvenile Artists Presenting an Electric Musical Toe-Dancing Novelty" act. They were playing in small spots near New York: Passaic, Paterson, Shamokin.

Frank Vincent, the head booking agent of the Orpheum Circuit, was the target of all these preparations, and when Austerlitz thought the kids were the best they could be within the limitations of their age and skills, he invited Vincent to see them while they were playing across the Hudson in Paterson, New Jersey. The combination of the Austerlitz charm and the act itself was enough to convince Vincent. He signed the Austerlitzes to a twenty-week tour of the giant Orpheum Circuit! This was a real coup for that time. Even the money was substantial: $150 a week, with travel expenses thrown in.

The Astaires now became, in the later words of Fred Astaire himself, an "important act." Indeed they were. They played Philadelphia, Des Moines, Sioux City, Denver, Butte, Seattle, Oakland, San Francisco, Los Angeles, Salt Lake City, St. Paul, Lincoln, Milwaukee. They even played their old hometown—Omaha.

The billing there was huge, and at every performance flowers flowed onto the stage. There was a little white poodle in one basket for Adele. The Astaires were in fast company on that circuit, and they knew it. They did their act, but most of all, they stood in the wings and watched the other stars—and they learned. The stars were such recognized names of the era as W. E. Whittle, the ventriloquist; Joe Cook, the comic; Jwan Teschernoff and his trick ponies; and Jesse L. Lasky's "Piano-Phiends."

With the twenty-week tour completed, the Astaires returned to New York and moved to Asbury Park to recuperate. The act was a success, and they were signed on immediately for another tour. Exciting stuff, indeed! Two years in show business and already a class act.

Austerlitz, who had now assumed the title of business manager for the pair, huddled with the booking agents for discussion. One of the problems with the act was its clumsy prop setup. For that reason, it could not be worked into many stage situations; certain very good spots could not be booked because of the equipment snag. And so it was decided to cut the act down to size—meaning, throw out the wedding cakes and gimmicks and retain the toe dances and the songs.

Young Fred was spending his time to advantage now, too. Having more or less mastered toe dancing, he learned to play the piano and took some singing lessons. Adele was already adept at both playing and singing, and she was a natural. Fred had to try harder. With each of them playing and singing, finally, the act had an added versatility to it. Fred also worked on the accordion and later played the clarinet for a short time.

It was during the refurbishing of the act that Fred began to throw in a few ideas of his own—a few of which were even incorporated in the act. Some of them were dance steps; it was a kind of beginning of a choreography career.

The second tour turned out to be as successful as the first, which was a pleasant surprise to the Austerlitzes, since it meant that there was enough talent in the pair to obviate the need for expensive and clumsy props and stage gimmicks.

Because of the streamlining of the act, the "electric" bit was discarded in the name, and the billing became simply "The Astaires: Songs and Dances."

It was a dizzying whirl, and the kids were enjoying every minute of it. Fred was allowed to hang around the theater after the act was off, but Adele was whisked back to the hotel by her mother. "Adele returned to her paper dolls, while I tried to further my ham education" was the way Fred put it later.

Vaudeville was not exactly a clean-cut life for a young boy to be living, but Fred thrived on it. The Astaires stayed in fleabag hotels sometimes, but that was plush compared to the typical show-biz boarding houses maintained strictly for the traveling troupes of the day. There were long, grueling train rides, with soot blowing back from the engine and choking the throat when the windows were open. There were lonely station platforms with groups of weary actors standing around guarding their bags or mourning over lost ones. There were grimy theaters, half empty, with acoustics that ruined everything but a shouted line.

The kids shared their lives not with their peers in a normal grammar-school situation but with clowns, jugglers, acrobats, comics, animal trainers, tumblers, contortionists, singers, bell ringers— anything that might fit the bill at the side of the stage. Some of these poor souls were on their way down after long and dreary years fighting for fame and losing; others were on their way up; still others were hoping and hoping and getting older every day.

Fred soon learned to view the whole thing with a sense of humor. An old saying seemed to sum up the life of a vaudevillian at the time: "Learning a lot of things but not getting any smarter."

It was Adele who carried the act. Fred was lucky to have a talented sister. From her he learned to face each new day with a combination of good cheer, vitality, humor, and tenacity in spite of his inborn pessimism.

Variety's "Dash" covered the Astaires on October 17, 1908, while they appeared at the Hudson Theater in Union Hall, New Jersey:

"The Astaire Children"—they were billed as "The Astaires; Songs and Dances"—"are a nice-looking pair of youngsters, prettily dressed, and they work in an easy style, without the predominating 'freshness' which usually stands out above everything else with 'prodigies.' "

Dash's statement evokes an era of mama's girls and boys all struggling for success in new and snazy duets.

"Dancing is the feature. It ranges from toe to the more popular (in vaudeville) hardshoe."

"Hardshoe" was the precursor of "taps." Dance styles were changing at the time in a revolutionary manner, as will be discussed in detail later.

"The singing," Dash's piece goes on, "falls almost entirely to the boy, who has a surprisingly powerful voice for a lad of his years. The girl's voice is light."

Vocals were new to the act, of course, but it seemed that Fred and Adele were making the most of a good thing.

"The boy sings an Italian song as a solo, doing rather well with it, although at times the value of the song-story is lost through an effort to squeeze in a bright line the lyric writer had evidently overlooked until too late."

Song pluggers were always on hand to give away songs to popular acts in the hopes they might catch on with audiences and bring in a few dollars.

"The toe-dance following the song could be replaced to advantage. It has a tendency to make the boy appear girlish, something to be guarded against. His actions throughout are a trifle too polite, which is probably no fault of his own, as he appears to be a manly little chap with the makings of a good performer. The girl, the larger of the two, does very well with the dancing. Her execution evidences careful training."

At the time of the review Fred was nine and a half years old. Adele was twelve. "Dash" caught the worm in the bud, so to speak. Although Fred was growing, Adele wsa shooting up like a weed and reaching out toward her teens. They looked almost ludicrous working together. Adele was at least three or four inches taller than her brother. Had their ages been reversed, they might have been able to weather the inequity. But to an audience brought up on the idea that the male is big and the female petite, their appearance presented an anomaly, an incongruity, in fact, a grotesquerie.

There were two worms in the bud, actually. Number two was Elbridge Thomas Gerry, the organizer of the child labor laws of the era. He was trying, along with legislators, to protect young children from being exploited by management in heavy labor, like working in the coal mines. The Astaires were not being taken advantage of. Nevertheless, the Gerry laws reached out everywhere, and into show business particularly. The age limit for children was fourteen to sixteen, varying from city to city. Below that age, a child could not be gainfully employed. He should be in school.

The obvious thing was for the performers to inflate their ages slightly, to lie a little. Fred even took to wearing long pants much sooner than his peers. At that time, boys wore knickers—knee-length pants that buttoned around the shins—until they were in their teens.

According to Fred Astaire's autobiography:

"I walked into a Western hotel one morning with my new long pants on and a traveling salesman clapped an eye on me, pointed to his bags, and beckoned. 'Here, boy!' "

Accordingly, Fred replied snappily, "Yassah!" Whether or not he picked up the bags and got a tip for his pains, as any self-respecting bellhop of the day would, he never said.

He did, indeed, spend a lot of his spare time with bellhops in the hotels he stayed in. He wanted to make sure he was getting the proper education a young man should have, and not necessarily a theatrical one.

The act was falling apart, anyway, with Adele so tall and Fred such a shrimp. When the "Gerry Society" caught up with them in Los Angeles, the Austerlitzes had been expecting trouble. Besides that, they weren't getting the best bookings anymore.

It was time to call a halt and take a rest.

A family counsel was held to discuss the possibilities. The obvious thing to do would be to repair to Omaha, their hometown, take a few years off from show business, and *then* go back to New York. Both Fred and Adele could go to school with their peers.

The result of that discussion was a decided negative.

"They'll all say we've come back to Omaha because we've failed," Ann Austerlitz decided. "That's not what we'll do."

It was the senior Austerlitz who finally solved the problem. Through his friend T. B. "Bernie" MacDonald, owner of the MacDonald Construction Company, the outfit that built scenery for Florenz Ziegfeld—and had, incidentally, built the complicated "wedding cake" props for the Astaires—he learned of the ideal place to go for such a sojourn.

Highwood Park.

This small community, the residential suburb of Weehawken, New Jersey, lay across the river from New York. MacDonald even knew of a small house that the Austerlitzes could rent. That there was a good school nearby was the keystone of MacDonald's suggestion.

Both Fred and Adele had been tutored from their youngest days by their mother. Having had a strict, basic, solid parochial education, she was a fierce but fair taskmistress.

"Except for two years in a Weehawken, New Jersey, elementary school while we watched for me to catch up with Adele in height, our only education came from my mother," Fred Astaire told a magazine writer in later years. "She taught us history, geography, and mathematics in Pullman cars and in boarding houses. The only other schooling I got was from talking to bellhops in hotels, but mother was the number-one influence in those early years of my life."

Going to school after settling down in Highwood Park proved to be a fun interlude to the Astaires. Fred had learned well at his mother's feet. Chronologically, he was in what was then called the fourth grade. However, it developed that his mother had done her work so well that he immediately skipped to the fifth grade.

Not only that, but Fred proved to be particularly adept at mathematics. He was also good at history and other subjects. He later felt that had he continued a formal education after those two years in New Jersey, he might have developed into a pretty fair scholar.

Although he and Adele had been isolated from their peers in the specialized hothouse of the theater, the two of them had no trouble fitting in with the people they met. Fred had his fights, of course; after all, he had been exposed to that kind of dubious camaraderie in the milieu of the theater already.

In those two years that the Astaires took a vacation from the world of show business, many things were happening in it. Some of them were big, and some of them were small. The biggest change was in the concept of the dance. Toe dancing seemed to be on its way out, much as "Dash" had written in his *Variety* review of the Astaires. The other phenomenon, "hardshoe," was evolving into something else entirely. That style of dancing was typically American, and it was now coming on strong, emerging from obscurity, into the big time.

"Hardshoe" was a turn-of-the-century phenomenon, rooted in the early years of the century. Hardshoe was not going to be called what we know it as today—tap dancing—until several years later. The term "tap" was actually coined by a Broadway producer named Ned Wayburn. The style of "tap" evolved from an early American dance called "levee dancing," developed way back in pre-Civil War days.

The father of tap dancing as we know it today was Thomas Dartmouth Rice, called "Daddy" Rice and also "Jim Crow" Rice—the later name became synonymous with social segregation. Other forms of dance—modern ballroom, with its origins in the aristocratic pavane, and passacaglia of Renaissance Europe, and the square dance, with its origin in Britain—were imports. But tap dancing came from American soil and is an indigenous as poison ivy and as popular as the ice cream soda.

Originally, black slaves simply used footwork that was the heritage of the heel thumping of their tribal ancestors. However, the rhythm they danced to was the basic American jazz rhythm. The body movements of those dancers were amorphous, shambling, and, above all, loose. Much of the time the early black dancers simply shuffled about in their bare feet.

This type of dancing was known as "levee dancing." The identity of the original dancer named Jim Crow is unknown. He may have been a Louisville stableboy from whom the aforementioned professional dancer, Rice, copied the routine, or he may have been a porter named Jim Cuff.

No question about the lyrics of the song that Rice wrote to celebrate this "Jim Crow":

> First on de heel tap, den on de toe,
> Ebery time I wheel about I dance Jim Crow.
> Wheel about and turn about and do jis so,
> And every time I wheel about I jump Jim Crow.

Blackface minstrel dancing started in U.S. music halls in the early 1800s, with "Jim Crow" Rice introducing the number between 1828 and 1831. He was not alone. A black levee dancer named Zip Coon was performing the levee dance simultaneously with Rice on the professional stage. Zip Coon's name remains known to this day in music circles. A circus performer called George Washington Dixon wrote a song entitled "Old Zip Coon," later retitled "Turky in the Straw"—a staple of early Western square dances, usually sawed out on a fiddle.

Both terms—"Jim Crow" and "Coon"—of course have been assimilated into the language as pejorative of black people.

Meanwhile, during the early 1800s, another art form of dance was developing in the British Isles. It was called the clog dance, invented by the Irish and brought to America by Barney Williams in 1840. The footwork of the clog was more complex than the footwork of the levee dance, but its unsyncopated rhythms were very flat. The clog was developed in 6/8 rhythm—a kind of quick waltz in half time. The levee dance was done to 2/2 or 4/4, march, time, or as it was called later, fox-trot time.

The black levee dance was the broken, restless rhythm of modern jazz, with contrasts of strut and relaxation. The clog dancer moved his body only from the knees down; the art of the clog was a purely auditory one: the more noise the better.

When *The Black Crook* appeared in 1866, it was a breakthrough as the first American musical extravaganza. It featured both clog and minstrel dancers. The cloggers wore heavy shoes with thick wooden soles and danced with their arms rigidly at their sides and their chests stuck out. They would sometimes dance on pedestals, making the clog noise ring out as loud as possible.

During the second half of the nineteenth century most of the minstrel dances had adapted the heel-and-toe technique of the clog and superimposed it on the levee dance. "Levee dancing" became the "step dance" then and finally the "buck and wing," which young Fred Astaire had learned to dance in his first years of training. Eventually the term "soft shoe" was applied to the mobile, eccentric "step dance" in 4/4 time. Performers used all kinds of shoes for this type of dancing, both hard and soft.

By now the levee dance had assumed its own image. It was distinguished by a kind of genteel humor in the performance, a certain delicacy and lightness of touch, danced to a smooth but leisurely cadence that sounded almost like a snare-drum solo. Both men and women learned to do this new type of dance.

In 1902–1903, the new hit on Broadway was a novelty act called "Ned Wayburn's Minstrel Misses." Wayburn blacked the faces of his chorus and used typical minstrel steps but added feminine gestures to the dance routine that evolved. To describe this new form of dancing—a combination of the clog and the old levee dance—Wayburn coined the phrase "tap and step dancing." From that moment on, "tap dancing" became the name of this new art form in America.

Actually, Wayburn's minstrel misses wore clog shoes with split wooden soles. There was no such thing as an aluminum toe or heel tap until about eight years later, in 1910 or 1911. But this American-rooted new dance style now sported a name that stuck.

The greatest of the tap dancers, black or white, was Bill Robinson, who appeared on the Keith vaudeville circuit and the Broadway stage during the first years of the twentieth century. By the time Robinson had molded the style into his own and directed it generally into what it was to become, most of the minstrel dancers had disappeared from the stage, and new dancers had taken over—most of them white-face performers. Jim Barton and Jack Donahue took on difficult dance numbers and performed with a sophisticated, light kind of humorous abandon. This airy style became the hallmark of the best tap dancers of the era. Pat Rooney did his high clog to a tripping 3/4 tempo—a fast waltz. Marilyn Miller and Ann Pennington, ingenious at the game, were as good at "taps" as the men were.

Suddenly the ability to tap-dance became a social asset. And suddenly tap dancing sold tickets to the theaters where the new craze was being executed.

All this had been happening during the years that the young

Astaires were getting started in their novelty work. Neither had really taken up tap dancing as visualized by Wayburn; that is, the Astaires were dancing not to syncopated rhythms but simply to the old straight dance rhythms.

Moreover, the very complication of executing the wedding-cake dances and songs precluded dancing to the more intricate syncopated style of music.

Word of the revolution in dance was of course in all the theatrical papers, and most of the performers were talking about it. While Fred and Adele sat in class in Highwood Park, the Austerlitzes were reading and taking notes on the new dance craze.

The schooling lasted for two years. At that point, Fred was twelve, "going on thirteen," and Adele was fourteen. At least Fred's genes had given him a push in the height department, and although he was nowhere near the equal of Adele, he was not freakish in size by contrast. There might have been some question about Fred's age—he didn't even look *twelve*—but with a little stretching, he could seem to be thirteen or fourteen. And that was only two years short of the magic sixteen.

Besides, it was time to get back to work. Ann and Frederick knew a good thing when they saw it: tap dancing was coming in strong. Plus a slightly interesting change of pace. A pair of dancers—Vernon and Irene Castle—had become the toast of the town with their sleek, neat, slightly oozy ballroom style of dancing.

Could the two types of dancing be combined by the young Astaires?

Ann visited the great man himself: Ned Wayburn. He looked at Adele and Fred.

"Let's try," he told Ann Austerlitz.

Chapter Three

"Do That Again for Me, Freddie!"

Ned Wayburn was indeed the premier instructor of the dance in New York at that time. With the success of the new so-called tap and step dancing, he was besieged by backstage mothers of all kinds. His school expanded dramatically. It got so big that Wayburn finally hired assistants to take care of the actual teaching itself.

He was a big man, a fatherly type. The Astaire kids never saw him but once, when he came in to one of the classes to see how things were going. He performed a little buck-and-wing step for his students, apparently to prove that he *could* dance. Fred later noted that he was surprised that such a big man could dance at all.

But Wayburn did keep tabs on his students. In an interview with Ann Austerlitz, he suggested that her two children would do well to take up the new tap and step dancing style. It was the coming thing, as everyone knew. But Ann wanted a balance, not a concentration. She pointed out that in a year or so her children would be old enough to dance together, ballroom fashion, on the stage. She wanted to get a free ride on the popularity of ballroom dancing that had come in with Vernon and Irene Castle.

Wayburn was impressed but was thinking along different lines. He saw the Astaire kids as nice youngsters and suggested that they concentrate for now on dancing, singing, and dialogue. In fact, he promised to supply a written act for them when they finished the courses they were taking.

Even though it cost a thousand dollars, Ann Austerlitz was happy to get the skit, since it was the work of an an old stage pro who certainly knew what would go and what would not. While Freddie—the name Wayburn called him—and Adele labored at their new "step dance" routine and practiced singing and playing the piano, the maestro wrote the skit. Ann paid him in four installments—$250 each. By the middle of 1911, the plot had been

23

laid out: It was to be about eighteen minutes in length and involved a young baseball player, "Freddie," his older sister, Adele, and their mother, Ann.

"You do not have to appear [on stage] unless you want to at the finish," he told Ann. He was using her voice, he explained, "to make the situation."

In the skit that finally evolved, the two kids are trapped in the house one afternoon by a rainstorm. Freddie wears a baseball uniform with "Little Giants" printed on it; Adele is in a summer frock. The boy is angry at not being able to play ball. Adele, practicing her music lesson, finally coaxes her brother to "play house" with her. The first segment involves Adele pretending that Freddie is her boyfriend coming to call. Freddie then shows how the boyfriend will act; the part ends in a song and dance.

Wayburn scripted Freddie to do a song. It was entitled "When Uncle Joe Plays a Rag on His Old Banjo." Freddie sings it first, then dances to the tune, playing the piano at the same time and letting his feet and legs do the dance and his hands and arms play the piano. This turned out to be a virtuoso stunt that usually got applause and turned out very well.

From this beginning, the kids then begin an improvisation imitating "mom and pop," with Freddie pretending to arrive home in a slightly drunken condition and Adele bawling him out unmercifully and endlessly. In this scene, Freddie wears a high silk hat that comes down over his ears and an old dress coat. This segment leads to the finale, with Adele playing the piano and Freddie again doing a song.

The gags were typical: Wayburn made constant references to the fact that Adele was taller than her brother, and Freddie played the drunk with the expected broad gestures familiar to the audiences of the time. In the drunk scene, Wayburn has Adele blatting along at a frightful rate, never letting Freddie get a word in edgewise. But Freddie makes the most of it, striking a proper pose as he tries to interrupt Adele but never really getting a word out. Then he strikes another pose, tries to speak, but fails again. Freddie had apparently picked up a thing or two hanging around watching the other high-powered comics working onstage. He knew when to pose and when to speak.

While not in any way a showstopper, the act was polished by the kids until they had it down as well as they could; then they went out looking for bookings. But they were still at that awkward teenage stage, and it was impossible to find any takers.

Wayburn used to showcase his students in benefit performances around the city—anywhere to collect money for this or that charity. He slotted his "Rainy Afternoon" skit into one of them at the Broadway Theater, and the act did well.

The *New York Morning Telegraph* said: "Fred and Adele Astaire are a clever singing and dancing team." Another notice read: "Credit a sure-fire hit to Ned Wayburn and those Astaire children, Fred and Adele."

On the strength of these reviews, the act was booked for Proctor's Fifth Avenue Theater one week later. Along with Loew's American Roof, also in New York, Proctor's was one of the most important "break-in" or tryout houses in the country for new and untried acts. Comic novelty acts were usually the most successful of all at Proctor's—Americans in tramp clothes, Englishmen with flaming red noses, fast-moving European acrobats doing all the tricks of the trade.

Here almost *any* kind of act would appear: ventriloquists, midgets, jugglers, bike riders, magicians, archers, shadowgraphers, dancers, opera singers, trapeze artists, minstrels. The Astaire kids were sanquine about their chances. They had an act that had garnered them good words in the *Telegraph*. Who really cared, as a mature Fred Astaire later commented, whether or not Wayburn had written those notices himself and planted them in the papers?

They opened on Monday in the afternoon. The Astaires rehearsed carefully, getting everything together, and waited for the curtain to go up. The horrible thing that made this otherwise dreamlike event a problem was that they had been given the first spot on the bill. They were the openers!

Not a very good spot for an act that was about five or six minutes of dialogue before the dancing started. No one ever got to a vaudeville house on time—afternoons were even worse than evenings. When the curtain went up on them, it was a disaster. The house was almost empty! They could see row upon row of empty seats on the main floor, and upstairs in the balcony and gallery no one was paying attention to the stage at all. Most of the customers were waiting to see Douglas Fairbanks, who was appearing in a sketch called "A Regular Business Man" between Broadway assignments; this was long before he went to Hollywood and became a movie star.

As the Astaires performed their act, the audience began entering in droves, banging down the seats, chattering, laughing, coughing— enough to blot out every line of dialogue emanating, or trying to, from the stage.

On Fred's solo, as he danced and played the piano at the same time, there was . . . nothing. When they finished, there was a bit of polite applause, but that was all. They were forced to sneak off in total silence.

It was not a happy scene backstage for them. But the worse was yet to come. After returning from a light supper, they checked the listing of acts and found that they had been removed from the lineup entirely.

"I'm sorry, kids," the stage manager told them. "Your act wasn't strong enough. You've been canceled."

"We were too young to know what it was all about," Fred confided years later. "But I remember my mother cried over it. She was very proud of us."

But at that point it certainly looked as if the Astaires were washed up. Nevertheless, some booking did come through—mostly three-a-dayers (and four on Saturdays)—nothing even halfway respectable. In Jersey City the audience even rained pennies down on them in the contemptuous gallery gesture of the time.

Nobody was interested in the Astaires except one man named Lew Golder. He was one of the bookers for a small-time outfit—the United Booking Circuit. The Astaires signed with Golder for split-week deals all over the country.

"We played every rat trap and chicken coop in the Middle West for about two years," Fred wrote in his autobiography.

It was once again time to sit down and assess the situation. The Astaires were going nowhere. As soon as the act had bombed at Proctor's, Frederick Senior returned to Omaha off and on to pick up a dollar or two selling whatever he could get to sell in order to support his family. So what was the best thing to do? Drop the act and go home? Or stay and keep on fighting a no-win game?

It was Frederick Austerlitz who finally came up with the proper solution. At this point, incidentally, he changed his name legally to "Astaire." That meant that when the kids came of age, they would be "Astaire" without having to change their names.

In his maneuverings, Austerlitz had met a vaudeville dancer named Aurelia Coccia and his wife Minnie Amato.

Ann was interested in the Coccias; their act involved ballroom dancing, in which she still had great faith. Coccia thought the Astaires had talent, but he also felt that their act and the execution of their dances were old-fashioned. He agreed to take them on to train them if they promised to work hard and practice, practice, practice.

Coccia taught the Astaire kids the tango, the waltz, and basic steps in ballroom dancing. Both Fred and Adele learned a great deal from him. Later on, Fred Astaire noted that Coccia was probably the most influential in teaching the fledgling dancers the steps that Fred later used in his most surprising routines. Coccia taught them that dancing was storytelling, that each move *meant* something, that there was romance in ballroom dancing.

Besides that, he hated the spoken dialogue in the Astaires' act, even if it had cost a thousand dollars! With the help of Coccia, the whole Astaire family scrapped the dialogue of the act and pared it down to what was then called a "song-and-dance" act. Not only that, but the songs and dances were totally reconstructed, with several new ones added. In two of these new songs, Fred was at the piano, playing and singing to Adele's dancing.

But Fred was also watching other dancers. He met Eduardo and Elise Cansino on one of their engagements and watched enchantedly from the wings, trying to pick up some of the Cansino moves to incorporate into his own steps. He saw John Bubbles, the great black tap dancer, who Fred secretly thought was better than Bill Robinson. He saw Bert Kalmar and Jessie Broun. He saw and marveled at Adeline Genee, the Danish ballerina.

"Almost everybody wanted to learn all the new steps," he said later, "from the bunny hug to the tango, and about the only way they could ever find out what the dances looked like was to see them in the theater.

"We made our own versions of the dances and put then into our act," he added.

Every time Fred saw a new move he liked, he worked it somehow into his routine. Most performers in those days set their routines at the beginning of the season and never varied them. The old saying "If it ain't broke, don't fix it" prevailed. Fred thought otherwise. He was, in the words of an old vaudeville friend, "never satisfied." He was the inveterate tinkerer—always practicing, always struggling to get in something new, something daring.

"We went through agonies finding the right songs and keeping them up-to-date, revising and improving the dances," he said.

The standard joint salary—for all the Astaires—was $150 a week, not too bad for the time, since many laborers were bringing up whole families on $2 a week. But of course out of that amount came food money, hotel money, costume money, and so on.

When Lew Golder finally got them booked into the Interstate Circuit in Texas, it was almost a breakthrough. They were raised to $175 a week. They were in the big time, all right, but still unimportant. They usually had the number-two spot—only one up from the murderous opener.

At the end of the Texas tour, the act was signed on with the Orpheum Circuit at $225 a week. It was in Davenport, Iowa, that the Astaires played with Bill Robinson, the great tap dancer. Fred was further interested in Bill because the latter was a great pool player and Fred had taken up this indoor sport on the road.

One night the two of them were out on the town and ran into a group of smartasses who were ribbing Robinson and Fred as they played. Robinson finally got fed up. After winding up two games, he turned to the know-it-alls.

"Take a look at this," he said, placing the eight ball against the cushion in the middle of the rail at one end of the table and the yellow ball in a similar position at the opposite end. He placed the cue ball in the middle of the table *between* the other two. Then he leaned in, ready to send the cue ball in another direction.

"I'll bet you guys a dollar apiece I can pocket the yellow ball," he said.

They all studied the table, then held out their money. Robinson went to the yellow ball and shot in straight into the pocket with his cue.

Pandemonium! "You said—!"

"I said I was going to pocket the yellow ball—not *with the cue ball*. Keep your money. And let this be a lesson to you."

Fred never forgot that one.

Soon the Astaires found themselves making $350 a week.

Fred later said:

> Taking advantage of the dance craze, we built an act that got into the big time. I knew it was the best we had ever done, so I wanted a stupendous name for it. I put in a great deal of brain work, writing hundreds of titles and threw them away. At last I hit it: "Fred and Adele Astaire in New Songs and Smart Dances." Somehow now this literary effort doesn't seem to show any touch of genius, but at that time we all thought I was a brilliant fellow and that it was a rewarding line.

But more than that, they were getting good reviews: Adele for her "comic ballerina" and "exquisite floating style," Fred for his "exciting agility."

Suddenly, in the 1914 season, the Astaires were booked at the Palace in Chicago. While not the equivalent of the Palace in New York, it was still a big-time booking. That was the good news. The other—they were in the number-one spot, their nemesis at Proctor's so long ago.

But the act had jelled, and the siblings were confident. They had lucked into a good novelty number called "Love Made Me a Wonderful Detective." Written by Tom Snyder, it was typically vaudeville stuff—special material for an act like theirs.

It started out with a nice dramatic setup.

With the music playing to a blacked-out house, Fred suddenly yells from offstage: "Stop! Stop! Don't you dare to move! You're under arrest!"

Then Adele, offstage, as well, answers by singing a line from the song: "What have I done to you?"

"Stop! Stop!" Fred repeats. "I've got you covered. See that badge on my chest?"

Now Fred pulls Adele onto the front of the stage as an amber spot reveals the two of them to the audience. And as the song continues, the two of them sing it. It was always a good beginning.

In Chicago, at the end of the opening song, the Astaires were stunned to hear a burst of clapping all over the house. As the skit continued, there were more bursts. And at the end of the act, the Astaires were called back to take a half-dozen extended bows.

Once they ducked out, the orchestra leader started the cue music for the second spot. The audience wouldn't have it. They shouted and stamped, applauding.

The Astaires had to come back and take another bow.

Fred and Adele had done it. In the parlance of vaudeville, they had stopped the show.

It was unprecedented for the openers to stop a show on opening night. All the headliners congratulated them, and that night they were promoted to the number-three spot.

And from then on, of course, they graduated to top spots and never had to play openers again. Oh, yeah?

The next week they played St. Louis. "Ha!" Fred said. "They'll have heard about Chicago. Wait till you see! We'll have a soft spot on this bill!"

They opened the show again!

"It was heartbreaking," Fred recalled. "*Especially* when we went back to Chicago later—and into the opening spot!"

In spite of the occasional setback, the Astaires were on the way up. They were in the big time, and they could now hold their own with the other stars of the era. They would summer together in Pennsylvania, where Fred took up golf with a vengeance and began enjoying life in general.

He was beginning to get around in the business, too. Always shopping about for new material, he began haunting the sheet-music companies on Tin Pan Alley. At Jerome H. Remick's, he made friends with a piano player and song plugger named George Gershwin. Gershwin confessed that he wanted to be a songwriter, and Fred confessed that he wanted to be a Broadway star. They both laughed at that.

"Hey, maybe we can both do the same show sometime!"

In fact, Gershwin was fascinated at Fred's piano playing, espe-

29

cially with Fred's left-hand work. In Fred's words he had a "knocked-out slap left-hand technique."

"Do that again for me, Freddie" was Gershwin's frequent plea, anticipating a much later catch line in a famous movie that did not feature Gershwin or Astaire.

By 1917 the Astaires were so hot they ran a self-congratulatory full-page ad in *Variety*: "Doing big in the West, what will the East say?"

Of course, the East—

In fact, the very next week the Astaires signed a contract for a Shubert musical show.

"We still didn't get to the Palace," Fred wrote in his autobiography, perhaps just a bit wistfully.

Chapter Four

Over the Top

At the time the Astaires "made it" to Broadway there were a large number of different types of theater in America. The most natural dividing line was that which differentiated dramas of the spoken word and those of the sung word. Theater involving the spoken word exclusively was called the "legitimate" theater; the term came to spoken drama from a historical period in England when all songs, dances, and musical accompaniment were forbidden by law, thus being truly "illegitimate."

The "illegitimate" theater of the Broadway stage during the second decade of the twentieth century existed in many different versions—some with little song, some with a lot of song, and some exclusively song, dance, and music. Music and drama were always intimately connected, even on the stage of the ancient Greeks, who to all intents and purposes invented drama.

According to the best guess of historians, the Greek drama employed choruses of singers as commentators on the play's action and the speeches of its principals. Drama dropped out of sight during the Middle Ages, although songs and dances continued popular with bands of traveling players and groups of entertainers. In the late sixteenth century, during the first blazing days of the Renaissance, the artists of Florence, Italy, tried to resurrect the classic drama in what was assumed to be its original state. Since any music that might have been used by the choruses in the Greek dramas that survived was irrevocably lost, Italian musicians began to compose their own. Thus, "opera"—now usually known as "grand opera"—was born.

It spread throughout Europe and became enormously popular, except in England, where the British seemed more amused than entertained by the loud voices and the extravagant gestures of the typical opera performers. Besides, the English language didn't seem to be quite as singable as the Romance languages. Shouting out emotional speeches in song just wasn't in the English tradition. John Gay satirized the development with his *Beggar's Opera*—an opera for the low-down and humble, in effect, and antiheroes and antiheroines of the era. Crooks and whores.

Later on, Gilbert and Sullivan continued the tradition of spoof, bringing the parody, or "send-up," to perfection. Other writers developed a kind of straight comedy without the heaviness of classic opera; this type of light story became the "light opera," or "operetta." Eventually, the operetta spawned its offshoot "musical comedy." Musical comedy became a Broadway staple that carried the theater through many of its darkest financial moments.

England had developed a tradition of "music hall" entertainment, copying it from the incredibly successful Folies Bergere in Paris. The music-hall show was essentially a long list of separate acts presented one after another with no attempt to link them together logically or dramatically. The French word "revue"—acts that were viewed again and again—was borrowed and used by Broadway to label this type of show.

Vaudeville, of course, had always employed this same technique. But vaudeville was different, inasmuch as a performance was never given an overall title. It was simply "vaudeville," with acts that were playing currently. Burlesque, which was a broader form of vaudeville, was essentially the same thing, really—a shifting bill changing every week or every other week.

The revue was a refined version of the type of show presented in vaudeville. Generally it was given an overall title to link all the acts together. But there was one essential difference. Most of the songs were written by the same writer or team of writers. The acts that did not involve singing or dancing were usually linked in some way to the overall "theme," or perhaps an act that was supported by a famous theatrical name might simply be slotted in without any reason other than the star's own clout.

It was, essentially, to this type of presentation—a revue—that the Astaires were assigned by Lee Shubert, one of the family of Shuberts who were to dominate the Broadway theater all the way up into the 1960s. Shubert was designing this revue to introduce a former Florenz Ziegfeld star named Justine Johnston. The musical score was written by Sigmund Romberg and Herman Tinkey. Romberg was a transplant from Central Europe—Nagy Kaniza, actually, in Hungary—who had grown up under the influence of Johann Straus, Oscar Straus, and Franz Lehar. Romberg was trained in melody, knew instrumental and vocal music, and was a musician steeped in the Romantic style. Although his parents had hoped he would become an engineer like any sensible son, he rebelled and took up music. He was later to write seventy operettas in America, among them *The Student Prince* (1924), *The Desert Song* (1926), and *The New Moon* (1928). Although in later years his music was looked upon as schmaltzy and kitschy, his tunes during the twenties were very popular and in general favor.

The revue to which the Astaires were assigned was entitled *The Nine O'Clock Revue* and was to open a brand-new rooftop, theater constructed on the Forty-Fourth Street Theater, just west of Broadway on Times Square. The policy of building two or more theaters cotiguous to one another—as in the current multiplex cinemas housed under the same roof—is apparently nothing new.

That the Astaires never did open in *The Nine O'Clock Revue* had nothing to do with their good or bad luck. It was 1917, and the war that had been raging in Europe since 1914—essentially Germany against the rest of Europe—had been spreading. President Woodrow ("He kept us out of the war") Wilson became incensed over the sinking of the British steamship *Lusitania* in 1915 and in 1917 entered the war on the side of the French, British, and Italians. Suddenly there was a feeling of battle in the air, and Broadway joined in fervently. *The Nine O'Clock Revue* became *Over the Top*, in honor of the hostilities in which America was engaged. However, the idea of a nine-o'clock opening was retained for the time being.

The revue included a huge cast of then well-known theatrical stars: T. Roy Barnes was the "featured" comedian. Joe Laurie and Mary Eaton were in the cast when the show opened, along with Ted Lorraine, Vivian and Dagmar Oakland, Betty Pierce, and Craig Campbell. Because of the change in title and the war fervor, there was a great deal of last-minute shuffling, switching, dropping, and adding. By the time the show was set, it had become a deeply patriotic, flag-waving vehicle dedicated to the "boys" overseas.

The Astaires had three dances. In the program they were listed under a rather oddly worded note:

> To Make the Lucidity of the Libretto "Conspicuous," the following Musical Interruption Takes Place.

Three of these "interruptions" were listed as dances performed by Fred and Adele Astaire. In one of them, Fred was listed erroneously as "Ted."

The Astaires did a dance routine to accompany Vivian Oakland in her song "Frocks and Frills," then did their own song-and-dance number "Where Is the Language to Tell?"

plus an ensemble number to the "Justine Johnston Rag" with the Oakland sisters, Betty Pierce, and Ted Lorraine.

Because of all the last-minute changes and the shuffling about of the material to make it a patriotic package, the show was very ragged at its tryout in New Haven at the Shubert Theater. What helped, however, was the very visible and vocal presence of Yale college students in the audience. They whooped it up for the Astaires and any pretty girl in the cast.

The show, still being revised and worked over, opened the following Tuesday in New York on November 28, 1917, in Times Square. The debut of *Over the Top* was also the formal opening of the Theater on the Roof itself, and it was a gala event. The nine o'clock opening hour was a plus, especially with the reviewers.

One of them, Louis Sherwin of the *New York Globe*, was very kind to the rather tacky show. "One of the prettiest features of the show," he wrote, "is the dancing of the two Astaires." He was especially kind to Adele. "The girl, a light, spiritlike little creature, has really an exquisite floating style in her caperings." But he had good words for Fred, too. "The young man combines eccentric agility with humor." Sherwin went on to praise the management for opening late, although he wrote that he hoped "for the sake of the customers" that the show would end at eleven, as promised, in the future.

In spite of that, the management of the theater moved the curtain time up to eight-thirty, a more normal hour, since business was not all that good. Sales, in fact, faltered. T. Roy Barnes was unhappy with the show and pulled out. He was a top comic of the day and did not want such a turkey on his record. In stepped a replacement by the name of Ed Wynn—later to be the Texaco Fire Chief on radio and television. The newcomer added a lot of life to the show, and his stunts and verve lifted the lagging production to a higher level of excitement.

Still, it was not a rousing success. The show ran for about ten weeks—seventy-eight performances, actually—and then folded to start its road run. One of the eastern stops was the Garrick Theater in Washington, D.C., where an interested spectator in the audience liked what he saw of the Astaires. He was Charles B. Dillingham, in the words of Brooks Atkinson one of Broadway's most "fashionable producers." Shortly after the show, Dillingham called in the Astaires and signed them for an upcoming show called *Apple Blossoms*, an operetta written by Fritz Kreisler, Victor Jacobi, and William LeBaron. This would not be the Astaires' next show, since the Shuberts had them signed on for that, but would be the one following.

In the meantime, the road tour took up the remainder of the

season, and the second Shubert show was in the offing for 1918. This was called *The Passing Show of 1918*, another musical revue with Sigmund Romberg numbers as well as some by Jean Schwartz. The Astaires got $350 a week, a raise of $100 from *Over the Top*. The format of this revue was similar to that of *Over the Top*, and the main plus was the presence once again of the redoubtable Ed Wynn as the star. In addition to Wynn, the cast included two very strong stars in Frank Fay and Charles Ruggles.

Fred and Adele liked working in the atmosphere of one of the Shubert shows. In addition to Ed Wynn, the two main stars of the extravaganza were Willie and Eugene Howard, one a clever comic the other a straight man and singer.

Adele had a solo, "I Can't Make My Feet Behave." So did Fred. His was "Squab Farm." They worked three other numbers together. First they did an ensemble with Emily Miles and Nell Carrington called "Bring on the Girls," then "Twit, Twit, Twit," and finally the "Galli-Curci Rag."

"Twit, Twit, Twit" was typical of the patriotic stunts of the time—corny but serviceable. Fred and Adele were dressed up as big birds, but with a slight difference; they were bird *aviators*. The lyrics went something like this: "Twit, twit, twit! You'd better do your little bit, bit, bit!" Fred hated the costume and said he always felt the fool standing there with Adele in front of a stageful of "chicks" behind him. Besides that, Fred was required to do a lot of jumping and flying all over the stage to choreography staged by the dance director.

In the ensemble "Bring on the Girls," Fred, Sam White, and Lon Clayton were supposed to be waiters in a Childs Restaurant. They did their dances sliding over long tables and serving up coffee and pancakes.

They started rehearsing in June 1918. The war in Europe was expanding, and Fred was in a vulnerable position. Voluntary recruitment had not reached expectations, and Congress passed a draft law in 1917. Fred was now eligible.

The show opened July 25, 1918, at the Winter Garden in New York. Heywood Broun gave Fred particular mention. After writing that the evening's entertainment was a combination of gorgeous sets, good songs, and a fairly dull book, Broun wrote: "In an evening in which there was an abundance of good dancing, Fred Astaire stood out." But there was plenty for Adele, as well. "He and his partner, Adele Astaire, made the show pause early in the evening with a beautiful loose-limbed dance. It almost seemed as if the two young persons had been poured into the dance."

What Heywood Broun had noticed in his revue was becoming a keynote of the Astaire act: their "loose-limbed" approach to the

35

dance. Adele was developing into a more than beautiful young woman: she was bewitching, as well. And Fred, in tune with the times, was playing the "cool cat" role that would become the hallmark of the 1920s Jazz Age. Of course, with the war still on and the attention of the country still pretty much focused on Europe, there was little time for people to see themselves and where they were going with any clarity.

One of Fred's actor buddies had a Stutz Bearcat and liked to ride around New York in it. On an afternoon that was not a matinee date, he and a friend took Fred for a ride out to Belmont Park. Fred found horse racing a fascinating sport and even took the plunge that very first time by betting on a horse that won at four to one. It wasn't winning the bet that interested him. He simply decided that he liked the sport.

It was the beginning of one of the big loves of his life. He attended the races from that time on, whenever he had the time and the money.

Although Fred finally was classified 1A by his draft board, he never had to report for duty. Armistice Day, November 11, 1918, took care of that. In six months *The Passing Show* finished up its tour on the road. Actually, it had been a very good run: 125 performances at the Winter Garden and the rest of the year on the road.

The show Charles Dillingham had signed up the Astaires to do in 1919 was *Apple Blossoms*, with music by Fritz Kreisler and Victor Jacobi. It was to star one male heartthrob of the era, the singing star John Charles Thomas, and his leading lady Wilda Bennett. What intrigued the Astaires more than anything was that their salary had escalated in this deal to $550 a week.

Kreisler, incidentally, was one of the most distinguished and successful composers and violinists of the era. Born in Austria, he emigrated to the United States to establish himself in the musical and theatrical world. From about 1901 he was the most popular violinist in the country. He composed a number of operettas, of which one was *Apple Blossoms*.

Fred later told of his meeting with the great Kreisler:

"Word came that Kreisler wanted to see me, and I went to his studio."

Once there, Fred stood in awe of the great man, who looked him over with amusement and asked, "What sort of music do you want for your dances?"

If Fred knew his leg was being pulled ever so slightly, he did not let on and started to hum Kreisler a little bit of a show tune to give him the idea of what he wanted. This teenage kid who had just escaped the draft telling Fritz Kreisler what kind of music to write! It could have been a sketch right out of one of the future Astaire movies.

Kreisler was playing the game himself. He pretended not to understand what Astaire was getting at.

"He didn't catch the idea," Fred said later. "Impulsively I sat down at the piano and played. *I* played for Kreisler!" But that wasn't the punch line. "And the tune was one of his own compositions!"

Who was actually kidding whom is of little moment.

"He didn't seem to mind my interpretation of his work," Fred concluded, "and a few days later [he] had not only composed special music for me, but, at the first rehearsal, he played it himself while we practiced!"

C. B. Dillingham thought it was a pretty funny situation to have Kreisler rehearsing on the piano with his teenage terpsichorines, and he called out to them, "Why don't you get a decent piano player? I told that guy to bring his fiddle, but he won't do it!"

Actually, the Astaires danced one bit in that show to Kreisler's great "Tambourine Chinois." They were scheduled to dance in two of the numbers: Jacobi's "On the Banks of the Bronx," with singer Rena Parka and Percival Knight, and Kreisler's "A Girl, a Man, a Night, a Dance," sung by Florence Shirley. There were of course incidental dances to the music of Kreisler, as well.

One day as they were rehearsing, a voice called out from the orchestra pit:

"Hey, Freddie! You didn't expect to find me here, did you? We'll be doing that show together yet!" Fred looked down and saw George Gershwin at the rehearsal piano. He had just opened with his first musical, *La La Lucille*, which he said was doing pretty well. They had a few laughs together before Gershwin left.

The show had its preliminary tryout in Baltimore and was an immediate success. On October 7, 1919, *Apple Blossoms* opened at the Globe Theater. The public and the critics were enthralled.

Charles Darnton, in the *New York Evening World*: "Fred Astaire and his pretty sister, Adele, danced as though they were twins and scored the biggest hit they've ever made."

Alexander Woollcott, in the *New York Times*:

"There should be a half a dozen special words for the vastly entertaining dances by the two Adaires [sic], in particular for those by the incredibly nimble and lack-a-daisical Adaire named Fred. He is one of those extraordinary persons whose senses of rhythm and humor have been all mixed up, whose very muscles of which he seems to have an extra supply are downright facetious."

Woollcott was not the only critic to have trouble trying to unravel the true entymology of the Astaires' invented name. Others than Woollcott, who assumed apparently that the typesetter working on the program was in his cups or overworked, decided that it must be French, and one once cheered "the Parisian chic of the young Astaires."

They were really on their way—nowhere to go but up! These were the happiest days of the young Astaires' lives. They had only two spots to worry about, and they were in the hit of the season! It lasted for 256 performances at the Globe before going on the road. They took full advantage of it.

"We went to many parties," Fred later recalled. "Nightclubs. In fact, all through those Broadway stage years, we did the nightclub thing a-plenty."

Later on, during his later career, Fred often thought that his early life might have been reason enough for him to shy away from the night life once he was married and settled down.

For the tour of *Apple Blossoms*, the Astaires' salary rose to $750 a week per contract. It was while on the road that Fred began polishing golfing game. He and John Charles Thomas used to play all the courses they could find anywhere they were.

In April 1921 it was all over. The next show was *The Love Letter*, with music by Victor Jacobi and book and lyrics by William LeBaron. Based on a Ferenc Molnar story, the book seemed perfect. The cast included John Charles Thomas again, Clayton Thomson, Alice Brady, Marjorie Gateson, Will West, Bess Franklin, and June Carroll. Alice Brady had made a number of movies in the past decade but had opted for the stage. Once sound came in, she would return to become famous as the fluttering society matron in pictures like *My Man Godfrey* and in Fred Astaire's own *The Gay Divorcée*!

All that talent . . .

For it was to be a loss all the way. Well, not *all* the way. It added one special bow to the Astaires' quiver. Rehearsals at the Globe Theater were going on one day when the choreographer of the show, a Britain named Edward Royce but always called "Teddie" or "Ted," was bemused as he watched Adele and Fred on the stage.

"Delly," he said, "put your arms in front of you. No, no. I mean, like you're on a bicycle holding the handlebars. That's it!"

A moment's pause.

"Now run around in a circle." She did so. "No, don't just do it. Do it as if it's *important*—as if you're intent on really getting somewhere."

She did, and it looked goofy to Fred.

38

Then Royce started singing, "Oom-pah, oom-pah, oom-pah, oom-pah," and Adele caught the rhythm. He told the rehearsal piano to do oom-pahs, and Adele continued jogging in a big circle about twenty feet in diameter. To Fred it looked as if she were a six-day bicycle racer.

"Freddie," Royce said, laughing, "you get there beside her and do the same thing! That's it—shoulder to shoulder."

Teddie watched, chuckling, and it went on for minutes.

"I think we've got something here," he said finally. "You can sustain that for four or five runarounds and then make an exit. I'll wager the audience will demand no end of encores!"

He was thinking again. "What we need here is a 'nut' number. Something dumb and nonsensical—an 'Owl and the Pussycat' kind of thing. Once it's finished, then you do the runaround and run off."

He told Victor Jacobi and William LeBaron what sort of song he wanted, and they returned the next day with "Upside Down."

In the end, the show turned out to be a loss, but the Astaires had a find of their own. They called it "The Oompah Trot" and, with revisions, used it as a standard item in almost every show they did.

As for *The Love Letter*—well . . .

The preliminary tryout was slated for Philadelphia in the Forrest Theater. It was only a fair show, although the critics liked it. When it opened October 4, 1921, at the Globe Theater in New York, it was obvious that the show was in trouble, the out-of-town critics too kind.

It died after only thirty-one performances.

Chapter Five

Lady, Be Good!

Alex A. Aarons was the son of Alfred E. Aarons, a principal executive of Klaw and Erlanger, one of the most powerful of the theater-producer–owner firms. Aarons had seen the Astaires onstage and had even talked to Fred at a time Aarons was selling ties at Finchley's men's store in Manhattan, in which he had part interest. His main interest, however, was in producing musical comedies. He knew George Gershwin, and he had seen enough of the Astaires to know that he would like to have them perform for him.

With the breakdown of *The Love Letter*, Fred and Adele were at loose ends by the end of the tour, and at that point Charles Dillingham had nothing new for them. Aarons sent for them, and once Dillingham agreed to lend them out until August 1922, Fred met with Aarons.

The show was *For Goodness Sake*, music by Bill Daly and Paul Lanard.

"What happened to George Gershwin?" Fred asked.

"He's working for George White on the *Scandals*," Aarons replied. "Can't get him for now." However, there would be three Gershwin numbers in the show, anyway, even if the composer wasn't on hand personally.

After the usual vacation, the Astaires started work on the show. The cast included Jack Hazzard, Marjorie Gateson, Charles Judels, Vinton Freedley, and Helen Ford. But the big news was that the Astaires were cast in *speaking roles* as well as singing and dancing roles. These were not by any means starring roles, of course, but they were the very next thing to it.

One of their numbers was an original dance that Fred rechoreographed from the "nut" number in *The Love Letter*. It was called "The Whichness of the Whatness and the Whereness of the Who" and was just what it sounded like—a "nut" number. Fred also kept the runaround gimmick that Ted Royce had invented for them, using it to wind up the Astaires' main dance routine.

Rehearsals went so well that the old-maid "Moanin' Minnie" began to suspect a disaster in the making. It was too good to be true. Even the dress rehearsal was good, and when *that* happened, so the old theater superstition went, watch out!

Adele shouted at him to look on the bright side, but he was unable to. He knew he would blow his spoken lines. He would slip on the damned floor. And so on. In spite of his worries, he did not miss a cue or a laugh. The show went fine—as smooth as glass. The audience loved it. So did Aarons, the producer. He admitted that openings frightened him; he usually hid out in the men's room until the final curtain.

"I feel like throwing up all the time the show is on."

Fred's father even liked it. "You surprised me. I didn't know you two could do all those things."

Although they were not the stars, the Astaires were signaled out for critical acclaim. In *Life*, a humor magazine of the time similar to what *The New Yorker* would one day be, Robert Benchley wrote:

> There isn't much to say about 'For Goodness Sake' that you couldn't say about most musical comedies except that the Astaires (perhaps late of 'Astaires and Down') are in it. When they dance everything seems brighter and their comedy alone would be good enough to carry through even if they were to stop dancing (which God forbid!).

The show was forced to close after 103 performances in spite of the fact that it was a solid hit. A terrible heat wave had descended on New York, and very few of the theaters, including the Lyric, where the Astaires had opened on February 20, 1922, were air-conditioned. As a result, most shows had to suspend production.

Dutifully the Astaires reported to Dillingham in the summer for their next assignment, *The Bunch and Judy*. With music by Jerome Kern and book by Ann Caldwell and Hugh Ford. Dillingham, always the kidder, started out berating the Astaires: "Now I've got to star you just because that silly Aarons boy gave you so much to do in that darn show!" And indeed they *were* starred in *The Bunch and Judy*. The cast was huge, with at least eight headliners.

From the beginning, Fred sensed disaster. The Kern songs were routinely good, but nothing exceptional. For one thing, Fred was required to wear a white wig with a knot hanging down his back. That was for the show within the show. For another, the range of a tune he sang, "Pale Venetian Moon," was too high in spots for his voice. The show itself was a bit vapid, as well—oddly enough, about an American girl who is a dancing star and who throws up her career to marry a British aristocrat. A bit of dramatic foreshadowing for the Astaires?

Worst of all, during the Philadelphia tryouts, Joseph Cawthorn, the costar of the show, broke his kneecap in a bad fall down an iron stairs on his way to the stage. Immediately a replacement was sought—but was hard to find. The opening was postponed, and finally Johnny Dooley and his sister Ray were engaged. The part was rewritten and split up into two characters, a brother and a sister. This required desperate measures, even though the gimmick of *two* brother-and-sister teams in the same show would seem to have been a press agent's dream-cast.

There was another accident during dress rehearsal when Fred and Adele, being carried on a table by a group of juveniles billed as the "Six Brown Brothers," were dumped onto the stage. Luckily no one was badly hurt. The only other bad accident was on opening night of the show. After that date, November 28, 1922, the show was known forever to Fred and Adele as *The Bust and Judy*.

On the plus side, the critics gave favorable nods. Heywood Broun wrote in the *New York World*: "Fred and Adele are the most graceful and charming young dancers available in the world of musical comedy. Indeed, the Astaires are distantly attractive even when they are not in motion, and once they begin to dance they are among the immortals."

Percy Hammond headlined his notice: "Mr. Dillingham's 'The Bunch and Judy' Is One of the Best." The lead read as follows:

> We do not recall anything recent in a musical comedy way quite so entertaining as Mr. Dillingham's "The Bunch and Judy." It seems to have about all the merits possible to exercises of its type, including a comparatively innocent libretto not devoid of sparkle. . . . The Dooleys and the Astaires are active and Mr. Kern's music affords its customary sweet compulsions.

Kenneth MacGowan wrote: "The Bunch and Judy luxuriates. There will be no other Globe show this year!"

But Moaning Minnie was right this time, and MacGowan et al. were off the mark. The show folded after exactly sixty-five performances and had a short road tour to boot. Even though the

42

Astaires' "nut" act worked—this one known as "How Do You Do, Katinka?"—Fred hated the wig he had to wear in that show within the show. When it was over, he blamed it on the wig.

For Fred, this flop was absolute disaster. His worst fears had been realized. Perhaps it was true that the Astaires simply didn't have enough pizzazz to carry a show. Here Dillingham had been euchred into giving them lead rolls—and they had killed the show!

In fact, Dillingham did not pick up his option on the Astaires' contract, freeing them for whatever their future held. That meant that they could go where they wanted to go, but in their case there seemed nowhere at all *to* go.

They had several local offers—one to dance at the Knickerbocker Grill in New York—but neither of the Astaires particularly wanted to take on that kind of work. They were in a position also to turn down an offer to return to vaudeville—at the Palace, yet! Viewed from where they were, vaudeville seemed a comedown. It was definitely down time for Fred and Adele. It might even be time for them to take a long look at themselves to see where they were, where they had been, and where they were going.

It was Alex Aarons who rescued Fred from the depths of his depression. *For Goodness Sake* was going to open in London, and Aarons had heard about *The Bust*. Hell, who hadn't? He offered them a contract to open the show in its London version during the 1923 theater season. The Astaires, with Ann in tow, embarked on the *Aquitania* in March 1923 for England. None of them had ever been out of the United States before. It was an exciting trip.

Both were dragooned to appear in the ship's concert toward the end of the voyage—a charity affair, of course—and they put on a show they were never to forget. The sea turned choppy, and when the dancing started, the decks were pitching perceptibly. This had an effect on their dance that added to its hilarity. In fact, since the entire idea of the dance was one of lighthearted youth, the response from the audience was unexpectedly warm.

Fred would later use the idea in the M-G-M musical entitled *Royal Wedding* with Jane Powell. He was one never to forget a good idea when it went over big.

In England the script was being worked on by writer Fred Thompson to Anglicize the American jokes and lines of dialogue. The title itself was changed from *For Goodness Sake* to *Stop Flirting* for some odd reason. The show was slated to open in the West End, but first there would be tryouts on the road to polish it.

After five weeks of rehearsals, the troupe opened at the Royal Court Theater in Liverpool, and the Astaires were astonished that the audience laughed in all the right spots and clapped at the end

43

of each number. There were even shouts of "encore!" It looked like a repeat of their hit in the States.

In Glasgow, the second tryout city, they scored again at the King's Theater. Fred spent the next day playing golf in the country in which it had been invented and in the next few days played all the famous courses when there were no matinees. Finally they opened in Edinburgh at the Queen's Theater for another good run.

On May 30 they returned to London to open at the Shaftsbury Theater. The crowd was well behaved during the first act. During the wait between the acts, Fred met with Aarons backstage.

FRED: Is this thing getting over? I don't hear much from them.

AARONS: I've heard favorable comments out in the lobby, but I'm going back to the men's room for the rest of the show, anyway.

But in the middle of the second act the Astaires broke it open. Fred and Adele had a dance together called "Oh Gee, Oh Gosh, Oh Golly, I Love You"—a song and dance—and the roof came down at the end.

"Encore! Encore! More!" shouted the audience.

And there was more to come. The "Whichness of the Whatness" and the runaround—developed by an Englishman, of course!—absolutely wowed the audience. With the "oompah, oompah, oompah, oompah" and the ridiculous, clowning runaround, the English took the Astaires firmly to their hearts.

They had curtain calls at the end, and Adele was forced to ad lib some words in front of the curtain. "My brother and I thank you from the bottom of our hearts and—and we want you all to come and have tea with us tomorrow."

Big laugh.

Fred was pushed out. He stood there, absolutely speechless. He waved a hand toward Adele. "She said it."

The Astaires were probably the two most popular American attractions that London had seen for a good twenty-five years.

Francis Birrel in the *Nation and Athenaeum*: "In their tireless high spirits, their unfailing delight in their own concerns, their litheness and unceasing activities, Fred and Adele Astaire ceased to be human beings to become, as it were, translated into denizens of an Elizabethan forest."

Sydney Carrol, in the *London Times*: "They typify the primal spirit of animal delight that could not restrain itself—the vitality that burst its bonds in the Garden of Eden. . . . They are as lithe as blades of grass, as light as gossamer, and as odd as golliwogs."

The *Pall Mall Gazette*:

They neither look like nor behave like ordinary dancers. Mr. Fred Astaire has both the air and figure of a highbrow. He has a bulging forehead and no display of chest or calf or anything of that sort, and wears a commonplace dress jacket all the time. Miss Adele Astaire is equally careless about appearances—just a romping anyhow with a happy-go-lucky manner, all temperament and intelligence. . . . Their final shoulder-to-shoulder gallop not only brings down the house but is one of the funniest things of its kind I can remember.

One thing put a damper on the triumph of Adele and Fred. During the long run of the show, Ann was called back to the United States. Fred's father, who had been ailing for some time, had become seriously ill. Ann reached him in time to take him to Wernersville, where she helped him try to recuperate from serious complications of his condition.

He died there. When Fred received the cablegram with the news, he was asked by the management if he and Adele wanted to close the show for a week or two.

After thoughtful consideration, Fred and his sister decided to go on with the show. "It was a tough night," Fred said, "but that was the only way to cope with the tragic news."

It set the pattern of Fred's life in the future, when the same thing recurred in a different and even more serious fashion.

The hit show was moved later to the Queen's, and eventually to the Strand. During the Christmas layoff the show played Birmingham and then returned to the Strand in March 1924. The London run totaled 418 performances. True, they were a huge hit in London—bigger by far than in New York—but they were still Americans, and their absence in Broadway show business was not making their audiences at home any fonder of them. If anything, they might well be the forgotten siblings of show biz.

But the social attention both Fred and Adele received from the wealthy young peers of the realm in London was unlike anything either of them could remember in the United States. The prince of Wales appeared at the theater several times, inviting them to join him later. Eventually they met Prince George, who became a close friend of Fred's. They even met "the baby" eventually—the individual who would become Queen Elizabeth II.

Reluctantly, they said good-bye to all their new friends in England and set sail on the S.S. *Homeric* in March. Aarons had told them he had something waiting for them to do. It was a show then titled *Black-Eyed Susan*—"That title is horrible and we're not going to use it"—but the entire score would be written by George and Ira Gershwin! Plus which, the book was done by Guy Bolton, an old hand at musical comedy, and P. G. Wodehouse, the author of the extremely popular "Jeeves" novels.

Aarons had taken on a new partner as producer in the venture, his production associate Vinton Freedley, the actor who had played the romantic lead in *For Goodness Sake*. The show looked like a hit from the beginning.

The story was a bit of piffle about a brother and sister who are dancers and singers forced to perform in the homes of friends who have a great deal of money and can spend their time loafing about. The sister pretends to be a Spanish heiress in order to collect four million dollars from a dead millionaire; apparently she gets it.

The Astaires were stars, but so were their costars. And what a pair of costars! Walter Catlett, an amazingly versatile comedian who later went on to motion pictures, was one of them. The other was Cliff Edwards, known in show business as "Ukulele Ike," a huge star from the days of vaudeville.

But it was the score that, well, scored. Once the Gershwins had their main song, they also had their title. And that turned out to be the classic standard "Lady, Be Good!" And so *Black-Eyed Susan* opened as the bright, marvelous, scintillating *Lady, Be Good!* Another of the Gershwin winners in the score was a bright, sparkling tune titled "Fascinating Rhythm," another all-time classic; that was a Cliff Edwards solo, perfect for the banjo.

Ironically enough, the best of them, "The Man I Love," was dropped from the show during the tryouts. It was just one song too many. As a matter of fact, the song later had another run of bad luck. Selected for *Rosalie*, it was again pulled before opening night. It never did make Broadway. But Gershwin was not disturbed. "The song is not a production number," he once explained.

It allows little or no action while it is being sung. It lacks a soothing, seducing rhythm; instead, it has a certain slow lilt that disturbs the audience instead of lulling it with acceptance. Then, too, there is the melody, which is not easy to catch; it presents too many chromatic pitfalls.

Chromatic pitfalls—that's how a classic is born!

The Astaires had duets: "Hang on to Me," "Fascinating Rhythm," and "Sweet Miss," which was the old runaround number. Fred had a solo: "The Half of It, Dearie, Blues."

"Hang on to Me" was destined to become a classic act, traditional of the twenties-type musical. The two of them are on the sidewalk just having been evicted from their apartment. Surrounded by their furniture, they try to amuse each other by arranging the tables and chairs as if the sidewalk were their home. Adele hangs up a God Bless Our Home sign on a lamppost. When it begins to rain, the two of them duck under a huge umbrella and do a song-and-dance duet to "Hang on to Me."

After four weeks of rehearsal, the troupe was off to Philadelphia for tryouts, opening at the Forrest Theater on schedule.

Aarons looked up Fred between acts 1 and 2.

> AARONS: The thing is a cinch. I just made a deal for six months with the ticket brokers in New York. We're sold out already.
> FRED: Did they have to come down to the men's room to do business with you?
> AARONS: No. When I heard those laughs Catlett and Adele were getting, I came out. Anyway, I'm cured now. I'll never be bothered with that sick feeling anymore. I've outgrown that stuff.

The show was a big, big hit. From the moment it opened at the Liberty Theater on West Forty-second Street December 12, 1924, everything was—coming up roses?

Arthur Hornblow, in *Theater Magazine*:

> The insouciant Astaires recaptured the hearts of New York. Adele is, if anything, more piquant and impish and her brother Fred more blithe and joyous. Their nimble feet twinkle faster than ever, and they came near carrying off all the honors of the sprightly new show.

Alan Dale, in the *New York American*: "They dance, they sing, and they have been jellied into some kind of plot which eludes me, as such plots invariably do, and I never worry."

The *New York Times*: "Miss Astaire in the new piece is as charming and entertaining a musical comedy actress as the town has seen on display in many a moon. Fred Astaire too gives a good account of himself."

The *New York Herald-Tribune*:

> Fred and Adele we salute you! . . . When . . . they sang and danced "Fascinating Rhythm" the callous Broadwayites cheered them as if their favorite halfback had planted the ball behind the goal posts after an eighty-yard run. Seldom has it been our pleasure to witness so heartfelt, spontaneous, and so deserved a tribute.

The show played through September 1925, then toured ten cities, winding up in London. Opening there on April 1926, it was another triumph for the Astaires.

Hubert Griffith, in the *Evening Standard*: "Adele Astaire is, I think, the most attractive thing on any stage."

The Daily Sketch: "Fred and Adele have only to appear and everyone is blissfully happy. . . . Their dancing was uproarious."

It was during the run of *Lady, Be Good!* in 1926 that the king and queen made one of their infrequent appearances at the theater to see the Astaires. That was an event itself!

When the theater in which they were playing was scheduled for demolition, they were forced to close in London but made a tour throughout the country, including Wales and Scotland. In June 1927 they returned to New York to start work on their next venture, a show written by Robert Benchley in collaboration with Fred Thompson and with a score by George and Ira Gershwin. It was called *Smarty*.

But *Smarty* turned out to be anything else *but*. From the start, nothing seemed to work. Even with the solid Gershwin songs, there didn't seem to be any life in the show. Everybody worked hard, and there were no slouches in the cast, but nothing happened. The title was changed to *Funny Face*. Still no luck. In Philadelphia the show tried out at the Shubert Theater. Opening night was much too long, too flat. The individual numbers seemed to go well, but the entire thing lay there like a beached whale.

Fred looked up Aarons in Philadelphia opening night.

AARONS: I know what's wrong with this thing. I knew after watching those two dress rehearsals last week. You're going to stay out on the road a few extra weeks while we rewite about two-thirds of it.

FRED: (big groan).

And that was the way it was. Benchley had to resign his task of rewriting because of previous commitments. Paul Gerard Smith joined Fred Thompson to do the resurrecting job.

The run in Philly was awful. There was no business; people had heard it was a dud. And the show itself was changing. By the time they reached Ford's Theater in Washington, D.C., things were totally confused. Some of the actors seemed to be playing one version and the rest another—or perhaps their own.

At this point there was one encouraging note. Victor Moore was assigned a part, and it was being carefully built up by the writers. This sparked some enthusiasm in the cast.

"In Washington," Fred told a magazine writer later, "we were playing one version and rehearsing another. Every performance was different from the one before it."

It was chaos onstage all the time.

48

There were times when I used to carry my lines typed on cards. I'd have to look down into my hand before I dared open my mouth. You know—look at the card—"and so-and-so, and so-and-so, Herbert," then another look at the card; then, "and so-and-so-and-so-and-so." Honest, I never thought we'd make New York. We even asked them to chuck the whole thing once.

On the last evening of the tryouts in Wilmington, Delaware,
Fred had finally had it. The tension and the agony of going through all those rewrites and recastings and so on were beginning to tell on him. He sounded off to Adele.

"I hate flops! And this is one. We might as well face it; this damned turkey hasn't got a prayer. I'm sick of this racket, anyway."

His valet and dresser tried to pacify him in the face of his antagonism to Adele.

"Now, Mr. Fred, you mustn't carry on like that. You know Miss Adele and you have been riding pretty smooth the past few years. You can't expect anything to be a hit."

> FRED: The hell you can't. We've worked ten times harder on this thing than any hit so far, and what have we got? I tell you, man, I's got de miseries.
> ADELE: Oh, let him moan. He loves it. This is the first chance he's had for years. Go ahead, Minnie! You know, sometimes you remind me of William Jennings Bryan.

That line broke up Fred, and he retired from the fray, chuckling
and shaking his head.

"That's where Alex Aarons and Vin Freedley were excellent managers," he admitted. "They knew, even when we didn't, that we had something, and instead of junking it, they kept working over it and over it until—well. . . ."

It opened in New York on November 22, 1927, at the Alvin Theater—a smash hit. The Alvin, incidentally, was named from the first syllables of Alex Aaron's and Vinton Freedley's names. They owned it, of course.

In *Funny Face* it was the strength of two solid show-stopping numbers by the Astaires that turned the trick. One of them was the title song, "Funny Face," and the other was "The Babbitt and the Bromide," the show's traditional "runaround." There were also two very good duets by Gershwin: "He Loves and She Loves," between Adele and Allen Kearns, playing her lover; and "'S Wonderful.''

One of the most spectacular of the numbers was Fred's appearance in tails in front of a big group of top-hatted male chorus dancers—a definite foreshadowing of his much later phenomenal success in motion pictures, the key dance in *Top Hat*.

Alexander Woollcott, in the *New York World*:

> I do not know whether George Gershwin was born into this world to write rhythms for Fred Astaire's feet or whether Fred Astaire was born into this world to show how the Gershwin music should really be danced. But surely they were written in the same key, those two.

George Jean Nathan, in *Judge*:

> The Astaire team lifts the evening as they have lifted equally dubious vehicles in the past and sends a show gaily over. If there are better dancers anywhere I must have been laid up with my old war wounds when they were displaying themselves.

Gilbert Gabriel, in the *New York Sun*:

> It's a light-hearted and light-toed musical comedy, charged with winsome Gershwin tunes, droll as droll could reasonably or seasonably be, and a rhapsody of the magical and flying motions of Brother and Sister Astaire.

In spite of its status as a smash hit, *Funny Face* closed in the middle of the summer as another unprecedented heat wave hit the town and the sweltering theaters were deserted in droves by the theatergoing public.

One night Fred got a call from Walter Wanger. Wanger was then working for Paramount Studios on the West Coast, although he was still basically an independent producer of motion pictures.

What he wanted was for Fred and Adele to make a screen test for him to show the executives at Paramount.

"There's a revolution taking place in the motion picture business," he told Fred—as if Fred didn't know. "With sound in, the business is going to be like nothing it ever was before."

This was a cliché so obvious that Fred made no comment at all. Adele thought it would be nice to make the test just to see how they looked. Fred worked up some enthusiasm, too. They polished up a bit, including a song from *Funny Face*, and under Wanger's supervision made the test in a New York studio.

Fred had no idea how their kind of dancing would appear on film. Nor did he know how his kind of singing would come over, either. Film was a whole new ball game. It was a different medium; and it needed values other than those of stage work. The change from legit to film had been disastrous for many Broadway stars.

Holding his breath, Fred took Adele to the studio where they had made the test, and Wanger ran it off for them. Fred began to perspire and jitter. Adele watched in silence.

When it was all over, Wanger turned to Fred. "I'm sending it out to the Coast."

"Don't!" Fred pleaded. "It's awful."

"No, you look good."

Adele had mixed emotions. She wanted the test to look good and thought that it did. Why not take a chance on it? Reluctantly, Fred finally came around to her side.

Wanger telephoned back later on, telling the Astaires that things were still "in the works."

At about this time, Florenz Ziegfeld called in the Astaires and talked to them about a show for the following season. But Aarons had already sailed to London to arrange dates for the fall of 1928 for *Funny Face*.

Nothing even came of the Paramount test. Rumors have it that the reaction to the two dancers was uneven at best. It was thought that Adele was fine but that Fred was not a fit subject for film. Because of their team status, it was known that if one was selected and the other declined, the studio would get neither of them.

Thus, the debut of Fred Astaire on film was postponed for another most important five years. That postponement may indeed have sealed the fate of Fred Astaire's future. The speculation at this late date is that if he had indeed been signed by Paramount and that if he and his sister had gone to Hollywood at that point, he, and they, might well have become casualties.

The particular type of musical he excelled at was not then in favor at the studios. More about that later. By waiting, it has been felt, Astaire was lucky, not unlucky. His career on Broadway was at its peak—with more big honors to come.

And something else—fate—was waiting in the wings, as well.

The opening of *Funny Face* in London followed the same pattern as *Lady, Be Good!*

The *Sketch*:

There is no mistaking the fact that London is about to enjoy another outbreak of 'Astairia' this winter. Adele's personality has still the same naive and easy-going grace, humour, and simplicity. Fred Astaire—that mild and intellectual looking young man—is still the mind of the dance.

The West End run of the performance totaled 263 performance, more even than the New York run of 250 at the Alvin.

At the closing performance in 1929 of *Funny Face* in London, there were several new visitors closeted with her admirers in Adele's dressing-room suite. One of them was Prince Aly Khan, probably the world's richest man and a member of what would later be called the "Beautiful People." With him came a good friend, a titled aristocrat—Lord Charles Cavendish. Cavendish seemed fascinated with Adele. Adele, used to admirers of all shapes, sizes, and kinds, was polite to him. Polite but reserved.

After the closing, Fred hung around in London and went out on the town with his many English friends. Adele took a week off in Paris. When the two of them met for the home trip on the S.S. *Homeric*, Adele told Fred that Charlie Cavendish had spent the weekend in Paris.

"He's awfully nice," Adele said casually. "He's coming to New York this winter on business."

Adele was a pretty good actress, but Fred could read her very well. *Monkey* business? Fred wondered.

Chapter Six

The Toast of Two Continents

By now the Astaire mystique—that ability to make a hit out of a flop—was well established. The two of them had been in show business now for some twenty-five years and had gone through all the awkward stages from childhood to maturity. In the meantime, they had become consummate performers in the arts of dancing, singing, and acting.

They were, in effect, the toast of Broadway and the toast of the West End in London. Everywhere they went they were surrounded by fans and admirers. They were featured in newspaper reviews and magazine stories. Although the media of the era were not so powerful and all pervasive as those of a later time, it would be fair to say that they were a "household" word even though much of the country had never seen them in action.

Adele's forte was comedy. Many of the stills around today show her either making some kind of delightful moue with her face, limbs, or body or acting in some way airy, whimsical, and just slightly nutty. Essentially, although no one had ever said it, she was the quintessential happy singles girl of the flapper era. Not a flapper herself, she bobbed her hair, dressed in the accepted costume, and played it slightly sappy on the outside but smiling and laughing on the inside.

Her piquancy and her beauty so balanced out her wackiness that the normal reaction to her, especially from men, was one of entrancement and wonder. She was as much admired by women, because she never played the aggressive, go-getting bitch-woman of the same era. If anything, she was a kind of stylized, elegant, and tasteful girl next door.

Fred's forte was support. For Adele's art, instinct, and intuition, he took care of the painstaking day-to-day preparations, the businesslike details that had to be handled, the complex money arrangements, and the logistics of their show-business career.

In addition, he was the creator and the innovator. It should not be forgotten that from almost the beginning, when they were children, Fred had provided the dance steps for their acts—he in combination with any dance director the pair might have.

Fred took his job of choreographer seriously. He was painstaking in his insistence on perfection. With Adele that was not a problem. Almost instinctively she fit into a pattern of perfection, doing the most difficult steps with an aplomb and dedication that would make one believe she was a hardworking hoofer in the off-hours.

Nothing could be further from the truth. Adele left the stage and floated off with some man or other, some women or other, while Fred stood around and agonized over some new turn he was trying to work out. She would be done with the theater as soon as the curtain bounced on the boards. Fred would have just begun his day.

Adele once discussed the way she and Fred looked at the art of dancing. "Fred is a perfectionist, which, I'm afraid, I am not. I hated practicing everything so many times, but he wanted it to be just right. I didn't care."

There was more to that partnership than a simple balance. Fred's main concern in life was to make Adele look good. He understood the male "supporting" role before it was a national mania. He fixed the dances so his sister would sparkle and shine. He was there to act as a kind of setting for the jewel of her talent.

Alex Aarons once recalled that Fred never trusted a property man to rosin the stage for him before a performance: He always came two hours before curtain time to attend to that detail himself. Lincoln Barnett once wrote, "Astaire was and is an almost masochistic perfectionist."

A magazine writer interviewing the pair of them for *Collier's* in 1928 wrote:

"Behind the footlights there's little to choose between the brother and sister Astaire when it comes to breeziness or juvenility. But offstage you'll find Fred far more serious and much quieter than his care-free, vivacious sister."

She went on to note that "the brother and sister are apparently quite devoted to one another, and Fred treats Adele with the brotherly tolerance that is the prerogative of brothers the world around."

Although Adele admitted that her brother might feel she was a bit trying and might sometimes almost hate her, most of the time "we get along great."

In describing Fred, the interviewer wrote:

"He's every bit as slender as he looks in make-up, with an engaging smile and an accent that shows only passing traces of the two just-closed years when he and his sister scored a personal, social, and theatrical hit in London."

There are, unfortunately, no motion pictures or tapes of the Astaires extant today from those triumphal years. There are only stills and memories of the lithe couple.

One writer said:

> Those who can still recall Adele as a dancer, remember her as a young woman with long slim legs, a flashing smile, and bold dark eyes. On stage she often wore daffodil dresses and face-framing hats. She had what has been described as a cooey soprano-like voice. It was *her* style that shaped the team of Fred and Adele, there was no doubt about that.

But it was Fred who provided the underpinnings. His sister set the tone, and he was determined to fit everything about the two of them to it. Although he was male in a macho world, he had always lived in the shadow of his talented sister, always served as the also-ran. He had learned the hard, bitter way that it was Adele who was the superior partner, and he had accepted that fact with a grace that apparently was ingrained in him.

Perhaps that was the reason his style always seemed to some as a bit too laid back—although that term was not in fashion at the time. In their book *Jazz Dance*, Marshall and Jean Stearns analyzed this jaunty nonchalance by linking it to Astaire's early defensiveness against his more aggressive and more accepted sister. "As he danced, he gave the impression of thinking, 'Okay, Adele's the star, so I'll help her out, but I'm bored to death.' And, of course, it influenced the development of his style of dancing: the fine art of understatement."

The reviewer in the *Boston Record* had caught this key element of understatement or simply self-defense when he wrote of the Astaires' vaudeville routines in 1916:

"It could be wished that the young man give up some of the blasé air which he constantly carries with him. He is too young for it and it deceives no one."

The blasé cover helped Fred play second fiddle when he wanted desperately to be concert violinist. But later, when they were the toast of the town—or when Adele was toast of the town—Fred shared in the accolades. As his confidence increased and as the hits continued, Fred found that he had accumulated a lot of fans himself.

In fact, in *The Band Wagon* he was to do a number called "The Beggar Waltz." In it he played the beggar to Tilly Losch's ballerina. She flips him a coin at the stage door, causing him to dream that he is a partner in the ballet they then dance. Fred successfully played on the audience's sympathies as the loser who suddenly wallowed in luck.

Later on, in 1933, when he was to open in his last stage role in London, James Agate described his appeal as "a sublimated Barriesque projection of the Little Fellow with the Knuckles in His Eyes. . . . Every woman in the place was urgent to take to her chinchilla'd bosom this waif with the sad eyes and twinkling feet."

It was a kind of aplomb, but a callow, collegiate, very vulnerable aplomb. That was the character and style of the man himself. His dance was something else again in technique, but every move he made was in support of this very effective stage image of sophisticated innocence.

In the late nineteen twenties he had begun to develop his own dancing style and assert a psychological independence from Adele in a series of solo turns that he wrote for himself to fill in show spots. And now he began to hone his blasé, carefree attitude into one of more substantial self-confidence. He began dressing well, began taking care of his appearance more, began practicing that "charm" he would later be so noted for.

Solo dancing is one thing—and Fred was beginning to catch on to that. He knew positively that one day he would have to go on without Adele. He could sing and dance, and now he could act. He might even have a chance to go on all by himself sometime.

A typical brother-and-sister act has one fault built into its concept. Although acting is make-believe, most people in the audience tend to squirm at the sight of a brother and sister even *pretending* to be in love—sexually—with one another. There is that old bugaboo of incest lurking in the back of most minds.

For that reason, the casting and writing of the various hit shows the Astaires were cast in precluded roles that made the two of them lovers. And since most shows depended on romance to carry the story line through, the stars generally had to be unrelated. Since Adele was the star of the family, it was always she who became the leading lady, with some other leading man cast opposite her. That meant that Fred was always second fiddle, more or less the guy whose subplot is there simply to play against the main star's.

Yet it was Fred who choreographed the dances that Adele did with her male costars. And he was learning to choreograph romantic numbers—but not for him and Adele. He began to see the value of dance as an instrument of love. Even in music, the lyrics of the typical love song tended to be extravagant. "Pardon my mush, but I've got a crush . . . on you," as the song goes.

He began experimenting with the use of dance as romantic

wooing—with the numbers he did for Adele and someone else. And he knew exactly where to go with his dances with Adele. When *he* danced with her, the mood was one of gaiety and fun, with never a hint of sex. Half the fun in dance for the two of them was to play out a duel the same way written dialogue exemplifies a duel of wits.

"We learned to insult each other bitterly and call each other harsh names—by footwork," Fred once said about the Astaires' dances. "We can dance with rage. But with the advantage: neither of us can dance like that long without busting out into a laugh." The comic duel, to music.

That fact was learned early, and Fred used it in his choreography during those years when he and Adele were moving up the ladder of popularity. For the two of them it was the perfect solution. It was one of the reasons their dancing appeared to be as much fun as it was to watch. The spectator could see the little nuances as they rat-a-tat-tatted at each other with their shoes. In short, they fought it out with their feet since they couldn't *woo* one another with their feet.

Florenz Ziegfeld was not immune to the Astaires' charm, either. He approached them with the idea of costarring them with his own big-time Broadway star Marilyn Miller. She was in Hollywood at the time, making a movie—it was a film adaptation of her 1920 Broadway hit *Sally* at Warner Brothers/First National—but she would be back in New York in time to get the new show ready.

Called *Tom, Dick, and Harry*, the new show would be almost everything anyone could ask for. It was an original idea that had been written by Noel Coward and purchased by Ziegfeld. Louis Bromfield would write the book, and music would be by Vincent Youmans. The lyrics would be by various individuals, among them Ring Lardner.

From the first, the show turned out to be hard work. There were changes and changes and more changes. The Coward idea was abruptly scrapped. William Anthony McGuire was called in to do a rewrite. The story now had something to do with a Salvation Army miss trying to buy her way into high society—and succeeding.

When the show opened in Boston for the out-of-town tryouts, it was a positive shambles. By that time, in fact, it had been been retitled *Smiles*—not in reference to the mood of the people in the cast, obviously.

A new song was added, something by Walter Donaldson called "You're Driving Me Crazy." Adele sang that song with Eddie Foy, Jr., also in the cast. Fred was given an extra number to do with Marilyn Miller. But nothing could save this turkey, Ziegfeld *or* Marilyn.

When it opened in New York, even Benchley was stymied.

Considered as the Golden Calf brought in on the Ark of the Covenant, it was a complete bust. Of course, no show with Fred and Adele Astaire in it could be really considered a *complete* bust. There are moments, such as when Fred is shooting down chorus boys with his stick, or, when Adele is executing the beloved "runaround" to the accompaniment of an uncoordinated French band, when the back of your neck begins to tingle and you realize that you are in the presence of something Pretty Darned Swell. Adele is a fine little comedian, and I don't think that I will plunge the nation into war by stating that Fred is the greatest dancer in the world.

Fred used the trick Benchley wrote about in his review later to great effect in his motion picture *Top Hat*, as anyone who has a television set or a videocassette player now must know.

In his autobiography, Fred Astaire told about how he dreamed up the idea for the trick.

The idea came to me one morning about 4 a.m. as I lay in bed awake. I visualized a long line of boys in top hats and imagined myself using a cane like a gun, shooting the boys one at a time and having them drop simultaneously with the sound of a loud tap from my foot, leaving a sight somewhat like a comb with a tooth out here and there. Then I behaved like a machine gun mowing down the whole lot of 'em.

Opening on November 18, 1930, at the Ziegfeld Theater, *Smiles* died mercifully sixty-three performances later.

During the life of *Smiles*, Fred got a call from Alex Aarons, who was mounting a show across town called *Girl Crazy*, a story about a dude ranch in the West. There was a dance number in the show written by Richard Rodgers and Lorenz Hart called "Embraceable You," and Aarons wanted Fred to help out with the choreography of the piece. It was being danced by Allen Kearns, the lead, and his costar Ginger Rogers.

At the Alvin Theater, Fred met Kearns and the young actress who was playing opposite him. They worked on the dance in the foyer of the theater, since all the other rehearsal space was taken up.

Like Fred, Ginger was not born with her show-biz name. She was actually Virginia Katherine McMath. From Independence, Missouri, Ginger was every bit as midwestern as Fred was. She took on her stepfather's name when, in her teens, she won a

Charleston contest and started up a vaudeville act with the help of her mother. The "Ginger" referred to her red hair; it was also a nickname for "Virginia." The act was called "Ginger Rogers and the Redheads." With it, and with her mother, she toured the Interstate Circuit in Texas—familiar to Fred, of course.

Moving to New York, and again with her mother's help, she got a job as a vocalist with Paul Ash's orchestra. At the age of eighteen, she won the leading role in a musical called *Top Speed* on Broadway. In the singing chorus of that show there was a dancer named Hermes Pan; more about him later.

On the strength of her role in *Top Speed*, she was signed to do a motion picture entitled *Young Man of Manhattan*, made at Paramount's Astoria, Long Island, studio. She had a nice line in the movie, typical of the times: "Cigarette me, big boy. Well, liiiight it!" She also sang a song: "I've Got IT But IT Don't Do Me No Good."

According to Hermes Pan, she was "the John Held Jr. Girl. She used to be billed that way in vaudeville, and it was her style at the time. She had those long John Held legs and real short, dark-red bobbed hair, and she used to sing sort of ga-ga."

Ironically enough, it was the popularity of the movie she was in that inspired Vincent Youmans to write a song *he* titled "Say, Young Man of Manhattan," the number assigned to Fred Astaire to sing and dance to in *Smiles*; it was, in fact, the number in which Fred shot down the chorus boys with his cane.

After her screen appearance, Ginger was cast as the lead in the Gershwin musical *Girl Crazy* in which there were some fast-moving and loud songs that she was not equipped to sing; her voice was soft and romantic. She was to do "Embraceable You" and "But Not for Me." Her role was split in two, with the other half singing the rowdy and bombastic songs. That singer was named Ethel Zimmerman—stage name, Ethel Merman. Her songs were "Sam and Delilah," "Boy! What Love Has Done to Me!" and—the blockbuster—"I Got Rhythm."

It was for "Embraceable You" that Fred was called in to help. After meeting her, he took her out several times and met her mother, with whom Ginger was living in New York. Lela Rogers was a look-alike for Ann Austerlitz, a backstage mother every bit as formidable as Fred's mother, although perhaps Fred did not perceive, or want to admit, the similarity. If he did so, he never commented on it. She was, in fact, a mother every bit as conscientious about a theatrical career for her daughter as Ann Austerlitz was about her own two children.

Even after *Girl Crazy* opened—it was a hit mostly because of Ethel Merman's key song, "I Got Rhythm"—Fred dated her

59

occasionally and took her out to a nightclub or a movie. At least she was in a successful show. Fred knew that at best his days in *Smiles* were numbered.

"I saw Ginger again a number of times," Fred recalled in his autobiography.

> *Girl Crazy* was nearing the finish of its long run. She [had] made a movie at Paramount's Long Island studio on her spare days and said she liked picture work. I told her it probably wouldn't be long before she would be a movie queen out in California. She was on her way to the coast in a few weeks.

It was Max Gordon who approached the Astaires after the windup of *Smiles*. He had a new musical in the works that would be directed by George S. Kaufman. The music for the show, entitled *The Band Wagon*, was by Howard Dietz and Arthur Schwartz. And the cast was superb: Frank Morgan, Helen Broderick, and Tilly Losch! Philip Loeb, John Barker, Roberta Robinson, Francis Pieriot, Jay Wilson, and Peter Chambers were also featured.

The Astaires immediately signed up, then took off for a joyful vacation in Europe, celebrating a change of luck. When they returned, they got to work quickly, and it was all smooth sailing from then on. There was no plot to worry about. It was a revue, just a number of songs, dances, and skits tacked together in no particular order. The numbers themselves were consistently good.

Fred had devised a new solo for the show in which he began the number by donning top hat, white tie, and tails. This was another shtick that he would return to in the future—it was, perhaps, *the* shtick in the Astaire bag of tricks.

The show opened to raves on June 3, 1931, even though the Great Depression was just beginning to get under way. Brooks Atkinson alluded to that fact in his *New York Times* review:

> Mr. Schwartz's lively melodies, the gay dancing of the Astaires, and the colorful merriment of the background and staging begin a new era in the artistry of the American revue. When writers discover light humors of that sort in the phantasmagoria of American life, the stock market will rise spontaneously, the racketeers, will all be retired or dead, and the perfect state will be here.

The show ran for 260 performances and was in every way a big solid hit. So good was the show and so popular were the Astaires in it that they appeared in an advertisement for Liggett & Myers

Tobacco Company's Chesterfield Cigarettes. The graphics shouted, "Good. . . . They've got to be good!" Adele and Fred were pictured in top hat, white scarf, and what appeared to be tails—in theatrical profile posed with white gloved hands pointing forward. The words coming out of Adele's mouth were "They're Milder, Fred." And Fred was saying, "Taste Better, Too!"

A foreshadowing of the 1980s Miller Light dueling phrases "Tastes Better," "Less Filling"?

But *The Band Wagon* was important for another particular reason close to Fred's heart. Adele had become engaged to marry Lord Charles Cavendish, whom she had met in England in the company of Prince Ali Khan. The marriage was to take place during the tour of *The Band Wagon* after it closed in New York.

The two would be married in England during the following summer. Cavendish was the second son of the duke of Devonshire, and the wedding would be an important one. The couple planned then to live at Lismore Castle, in Ireland, part of the family estate.

It was during the run in New York of *The Band Wagon* that the Astaires appeared in a two-reel short subject, made in New York for Vitaphone Studios. This turned out to be the only film Adele ever appeared in. Astaire never mentioned this short subject in his autobiography. Perhaps he did not remember it, or perhaps he did not choose to remember it. He was once asked how he thought he would register on film, and he replied:

It never occurred to me that I was anything the movies could use. I had a pretty good smile, which I had heard was one of the essentials in pictures, but an inventory of my face would disclose no feature which could be hailed as what the successful movie star should wear.

From all accounts, this two-reel short has been lost. Vitaphone became part of Warner Brothers, which was part of First National, and in the many merges and restructurings, much of the early film stock was lost. It was the only appearance Adele ever made in front of motion-picture cameras except for the screen test that had apparently vanished into limbo at Paramount in 1928.

With Adele's retirement and marriage, Fred was on his own. He was somewhat disconcerted, although he continued to be his usual ebullient, self-confident self to the outside world. Even at the beginning of the run of *The Band Wagon* he had been aware that Adele would be making her last appearance with him in this show. Because the format was a revue, Fred and Adele did a great many things besides dance. The skits were varied, and Fred asked for and was given a wide assortment of character parts to play throughout the show.

The morning after the opening of the show, this fact was noted by several of the reviewers, who had special words of praise for the unexpected comedic talents revealed by Fred Astaire's "new" look.

The story went around town that when Fred walked into the Lambs Club that evening, he was greeted with the rasping wisecrack "Boy, I hear you're an actor!" from one of the *real* Broadway actors.

Even so, there was no big rush to draft him for the screen. He had a good place on Broadway, anyway. What was the sense of changing? His appeal was really a "class" appeal, something that didn't really go over in the Hollywood offerings of the time. Maybe New York debutantes adored him, but could he charm stenographers, secretaries, and shopgirls?

In May 1932, Adele was married to Lord Charles Cavendish and went to Ireland to live. She had "retired" from show business on March 5, 1932, at the Illinois Theater in Chicago. Because of his commitments to the show, Fred was unable to be at the wedding in England.

"She was a great artist," he said of his sister, "incomparable and inimitable, and the grandest sister anybody could have. We had a million laughs together in our career."

When *The Band Wagon* completed its long road run, Fred was at loose ends. He sailed for Europe, first to see Adele at Lismore Castle, then on to the Continent.

Although he would not admit it to himself, he was frightened. He had to go on by himself now. He could certainly do it, but he had spent all his life in association with his sister. He would miss her, certainly. More than that, could he survive without her? Would the public, in fact, *allow* him to survive without her?

"Now I was on my own," he said later. "It was important, I thought, to prove to myself and to audiences that I could get along without Adele." It was at this point, on returning to New York, that Dwight Wyman and Tom Weatherly approached Fred about a new "intimate-type musical" entitled *The Gay Divorce*. The story had been written by Dwight Taylor, the son of Laurette Taylor and Charles Taylor. It was essentialy a farce about a woman's attempt to arrange a divorce. Fred thought the script needed work. As yet, no one had been set to do the songs.

Soon afterward the producers secured Cole Porter for the music. Porter, one of the top songwriters in the business, had a few numbers already worked up. He played one of them for Fred. It was called "After You, Who?" Fred fell in love with it. The implications of the title itself seemed to fit his plight.

By the time Fred agreed to do the show, Porter was hard at

work on another number, this one especially tailored to Fred's voice and style. The title was "Night and Day." Porter had the tune, but the lyrics were a problem. The story went that at a luncheon during a rainstorm at Mr. and Mrs. Vincent Astor's mansion, he heard his hostess complaining about a broken eave on the house:

"That drip, drip, drip, is driving me mad!"

Porter's eye lit up. "I think that will work!"

Later, Porter said the tune was inspired by a Mohammedan call to worship he had heard in Morocco. He said the same thing about the inspiration for "What Is This Thing Called Love?" and perhaps other songs, as well. Maybe it inspired all of them.

"Night and Day" was a departure from the norm even for Porter, who frequently went his own way. The usual format for any pop song of the era was thirty-two measures of music, broken up into eight-measure phrases: AABA, or ABAB, the letter referring to each musical phrase. Thus, the typical pop tune started with an eight-measure figure, repeated it, broke in against it with a "release," and then returned to the original figure. The alternate form, ABAB, was simply one musical figure of eight measures, followed by another, the first repeated, and then the second.

The tune Porter had written for Fred followed the second format, ABAB, for thirty-two measures. But Porter was only beginning. After ABAB, he added C, a brand-new figure that played against the first two figures, and then returned to B to wind up the song. ABABCB. It was a forty-eight-measure song—unheard of! Plus which, the tune itself extended up and down an octave and a half—twelve full steps!—rather than the conventional maximum eight.

But once the words were written, Fred realized what he had—a throbbing, haunting, *demanding* love song: a song of yearning, of need, of compulsion. Immediately he began work on the choreography, realizing that for the first time he would express in dance the give-and-take of a romantic seduction. No words except the words of the song. Just dance.

By now the actress Claire Luce, who later called herself Claire Booth Luce, was cast to play opposite him. She was smooth, svelte, and glistening—quite the opposite in some ways to the bouncy, spritely, and vivacious Adele. But in a way she proved to be the perfect foil for Fred in his new Adeleless image. To Adele's pert, lively coquettishness, Claire Luce was slick, sleek, and reserved—almost the epitome of the ice-maiden type that had become popular in the Hollywood films of the time, epitomized by the cool, icy demeanor of platinum-blond Jean Harlow.

Fred spoke of the show later with typical Astaire understatement: *"The Gay Divorce*, containing a good part for me, seemed to be just the thing." With that role he would be testing his mettle. And if the way "Night and Day" was developing meant anything, it would be his tour de force and perhaps personal stardom for himself.

Lead male lover was a role he had never before played. As the main romantic in the cast, he found that he had to change his sights just a bit to build his dance numbers. The dancing he could control, the singing he could excel at, thanks to the marvelous Porter tunes being written, and the dialogue was exceptionally good in spite of the frail plot to which it was attached.

To elaborate a bit, the story concerned an unhappily married woman who has hired a corespondent to help her in a divorce action. Through the ancient but serviceable plot device of mistaken identity, she assumes that the character played by Fred Astaire, that of a writer, is the corespondent, although he is not and has instead fallen in love with her at first sight.

Concentrating especially on the choreography of "Night and Day," Fred worked out all his dance numbers either himself or with the help of dance directors Carl Randall and Barbara Newberry. The overall director of the show, Howard Lindsay, knew Fred's work, and the two were continually in complete accord.

The dance Fred came up with for "Night and Day" is one of seduction pure and simple. At the opening, the woman is annoyed at the man's attentions and tries several times to escape from him. At one point she shoves him away from her and sends him staggering back across the floor. But he encircles her again, blocking her exit, weaving a spell around her in an obvious dance of desire.

She tries again and again to escape but is unable to. Her defenses weaken. She loses her will to go. Meanwhile, he mesmerizes her with his movements. She is finally won. The scene is as complete in itself as a scene of dialogue would have been. Fred's conception was to make it so much a part of the story itself that it could never have been removed without leaving a noticeable gap in the story.

Fred knew that this time he was saying something—something new and vital in dance. More than ever before, he was *saying* something about sex in this routine. He would survive or expire on this one! It was a new nuance for a Broadway show; most numbers, in particular, dances, had almost nothing to do with the story line except to give the dancer an excuse to dance.

Fred's choreography for the finale of the show was on the daring side, too. It was a spectacular climax as the two leads waltzed around the room at top speed, leaping over chairs and

With his sister and longtime dancing partner Adele, seen here around 1926.

Fred and his bride in 1933 about to board a plane at Newark Airport bound for Hollywood where they were to combine honeymoon and business. This was the trip when the entertainer made his Hollywood screen début.

Astaire and Eleanor Powell settling into a dance routine in the 1940 MGM film "Broadway Melody" for which Cole Porter wrote the music.

Dancing with Ginger Rogers in a scene from Irving Berlin's "Top Hat", 1935.

Lord and Lady Charles Cavendish seen here in 1936 visiting Fred
Astaire. Lady Cavendish, formerly Adele Astaire (Fred's sister) of the
New York and London stage opportunely made the acquaintance of her
young nephew, Fred Astaire Jr, just two weeks old, on this visit to
Hollywood.

With Paulette Goddard in the 1940 Paramount picture ''Second Chorus.''

Fred Astaire and Rita Hayworth in "You were never lovelier" released in 1942 by Columbia Pictures.

Joan Leslie is seen here in the 1943 RKO film "The Sky's the Limit." The young actress, whose 'glamour' was 'built down' for her part as wife in "Sergeant York," here enters the ranks of cinema beauties to have danced across the silver screen with the legendary Astaire.

With Judy Garland at the star-studded Hollywood Studio Luncheon in February, 1949 at the time of working on "Easter Parade."

With Cyd Charisse in Cole Porter's "Silk Stockings," (MGM, 1957).

Leslie Caron and Fred Astaire in a scene from Johnny Mercer's "Daddy Long Legs" (Twentieth Century-Fox, 1959).

Fred Astaire and Dinah Shore holding the Emmies they won at the Television Academy's annual awards ceremony in Hollywood, May 6, 1959. Astaire collected the largest number of Emmies in the Academy's history for his telecast "An Evening with Fred Astaire." Shore, a repeat winner, was named best actress in a musical series.

Ava Gardner seen here with Fred Astaire in Stanley Kramer's 1959 film "On the Beach" which was Astaire's first dramatic screen role. The film also starred Gregory Peck.

In a rare family portrait, Astaire with his son Fred, Jr, 23 and daughter Ava, 16, posing for the cameras during a break in the filming of "Man on a Bicycle," a General Electric Theater program aired on CBS-TV in January 1959 in which Astaire played the starring role.

Gene Kelly and Fred Astaire arriving at the Festival Palace for the presentation of ''That's Entertainment, Part 2'' which opened the 30th Cannes International Film Festival, May 13, 1976.

With his wife Robyn at their Beverly Hills home in 1984.

walking across tables, as if they were all part of the floor. It was a dangerous climax for the show but an exciting and memorable one. Both dancers fell more than once during rehearsals. And during performances, too.

The tryout in Boston occurred at the Wilbur Theater. In spite of the songs and the dances, the critics quickly spotted book trouble. And more than that, they leveled their criticism at the Adelelessness of Astaire:

The Boston Transcript: "An Astaire must dance and still does very well—but not for the general good is he now sisterless."

The Boston Post: " 'Gay Divorce' is what might be terms light-waisted."

Fred was despondent—and morose. If he could not go it on his own, what was he good for?

They played three nights in New Haven when things looked a little better, and by the time they opened at the Ethel Barrymore Theatre in New York, there were high hopes for the production.

The show bowed November 29, 1932. But the reviews—the reviews!

Mark Barron: "As an actor and as a singer, Astaire does not approach the perfection he achieves with his feet. In 'The Gay Divorce,' it must be recorded he has perhaps taken on too much of a task."

Another: "Fred Astaire stops every now and then to look off-stage towards the wings as if he were hoping his titled sister, Adele, would come out and rescue him."

Harold Lockridge, the *New York Sun*: "Fred Astaire, when his miraculous feet are quiet, gives a curious impression of unemployment."

John Mason Brown: "Dull . . . disappointment."

One critic wrote: " 'The Gay Divorce' received a tremendous reception on opening night due to the brandied roaring of Cole Porter's friends."

Another one: "Two Astaires are better than one."

And yet another: "Astaire is quite unattractive physically and would not look out of place jerking soda in a prairie-town drugstore."

They were not all negative. Brooks Atkinson, in the *New York Times*:

> In the refulgent Claire Luce, Fred Astaire has found a partner who can match him step for step, and who flies over the furniture in his company without missing a beat. As a solo dancer Mr. Astaire stamps out his accents with that lean, nervous agility that distinguishes his craftsmanship, and he has invented turns that abound in graphic portraiture. But some

of us cannot help feeling that the joyousness of the Astaire team is missing now that the team has parted.

Fred was nettled at his inability to make this show into the big hit he wanted and needed so desperately. It was successful, but only just. By throwing the upstairs parts of the theater open to cut-rate tickets, the sales picked up after a few weeks. In the end, the show played 248 performances—not a bad run at all.

But Fred needed something spectacular to turn his luck around. He was alone now, and he needed to get back his confidence in himself.

"It seemed as if my luck had gone away with Adele," he admitted ruefully. He had wanted initial acceptance. "But for once the public didn't believe the critics," he pointed out, "and *The Gay Divorce* ran for thirty-two weeks."

Not only that, but the spectacular staging of "Night and Day," and Fred's rendition of it, brought it to public attention, and within a few months it was the top-selling piece of sheet music in the land. By then it had been picked up by radio stations and was rapidly becoming a favorite on the air.

About this time Fred confessed to Lucius Beebe in an interview in the *Herald-Tribune*:

> The stage is beginning to worry me a bit. Just why I cannot say, only perhaps it's getting on my nerves. I don't know what I'm going to do about it either. I feel that I ought to dance just as long as I'm able to do it and get away with it. Lots of people seem to like it and would be disappointed if I should turn to anything else.

The "anything else" he turned to had nothing whatever to do with the dance world or the world of show business.

Interlude

Change Partners

One of the many perquisites of working in show business was—and is today—that performers of the magnitude and accomplishment of Fred and Adele Astaire could always associate with rich and poor alike. The status of performer is in effect a carte blanche of entry into all levels of society. And "rich" included those of a completely different life-style, such as the bluebloods that America was supposed not to have but did in reality have and revered.

Adele had been used to hobnobbing with figures from the highest levels of society in both the United States and in England. So had Fred. In America, stars of their caliber were regularly entertained by the rich and famous. Among the hosts and hostesses that routinely invited the Astaires to their summer places was Mr. Graham Fair Vanderbilt.

One Sunday afternoon Fred was out on her Long Island estate at a party, playing golf, which had become one of his favorite pastimes. The Vanderbilt place sported a private golf course that was one of the choice runs in the East. Tournaments, complete with prize cups, were mounted for friends and associates.

It was there that Fred met Phyllis Livingston Potter. He had seen her before at Belmont Park at the races, where she was pointed out to him. She was the niece of Henry W. Bull, the president of the Turf and Field Club. He had never been introduced formally to her. Fred was, incidentally, one of the few "show-biz" types who had been invited to *belong* to the Turf and Field Club. He was an "in" person.

When Fred asked Phyllis Potter if he could "call her for a date," she told him she would be out of town but was coming back in five days. When she returned, they met after the theater with some mutual friends. Fred discovered that he was, in the term of the era, "smitten." In those days it was unusual for a man of Fred's stature in the professional world, particularly at his age, to be still roaming about loose and single.

Of course, in his case, the fact that professionally he was partnered by his sister had something to do with his continued freedom and single blessedness. Now, however, he decided he was in love with this woman and would try to find out whether or not she reciprocated his feelings.

Phyllis was newly divorced at the time. The daughter of Dr. Howard Baker, a member of one of the most aristocratic families in Boston, she had married Eliphalet Nott Potter, Jr., in 1927. In 1932 she was divorced in the traditional fashion of the day: by staying the allotted time in Reno.

However, there was a son, and as yet the courts had not made up their mind who was to get custody of him. This custody battle was being fought in the New York courts. The son's name was Eliphalet Nott Potter III, but he was always "Peter" in the family.

Apparently Fred charmed Phyllis enough at the time for her to invite him out for tea the next day to meet her son.

"Anything and everything about Phyllis was first and foremost with me. I was gone." That quote comes from Fred's autobiography. It summed up the situation. He was sure; she was not.

Soon Fred met Phyllis's aunt, Maud Bull. Phyllis had been brought up by the Bulls. From his association with the Turf and Field Club, Fred had already met her uncle.

At the time Fred was rolling along on Broadway in the closing days of *The Band Wagon*. Learning to his surprise and chagrin that Phyllis had never seen him onstage, he kept urging her to come see him perform—to see what had made him important enough to be able to meet her in the first place.

After the show she did what she had promised Fred to do: She came backstage with her friends. Fred stood around and smiled until his face cracked, waiting for her judgment of his dancing, singing, and acting abilities. Nothing from her.

He suffered all the gabble and the laughs and the jokes, still standing first on one foot and then on the other like a love-struck teenager until he could hold it in no longer.

"Well, all right," he blurted out finally. "How was I?"

"Oh, you were very good!" she told him with a big smile.

During the trauma of his imminently ending partnership with Adele, Fred found that Phyllis was always a constant comfort to him. She got along well with Adele, and Adele liked her, too. Yet of course at that time there was no indication of what the future would hold for the three of them.

While going through the nasty custody battle with her former husband over her son, Phyllis was frequently depressed and unable to cope with the difficulties of the conflict. Fred tried to help her as much as he could simply by trying to cheer her up.

She was at his side, too, when the critics hopped on him for his work in *The Gay Divorce*. Throughout the tryouts in Boston and New Haven, he was on the phone constantly to her, telling her the details of the problems. She would laugh with him and sigh, and in the end, she would always tell him: "Don't worry."

Oddly enough, he stopped worrying. He, Moaning Minnie!

When the show opened in New York, she sailed back into the dressing room after the final curtain with a crowd of her friends to pick him up for a party.

PHYLLIS: What a *dreadful* audience!
FRED: So is the show.
PHYLLIS: I liked some of it.

With the final ending of the Adele-Fred professional partnership, with the growing interest in Phyllis Potter, with the tough problem of establishing himself as a dominant leading man on the stage—with all these cross-currents buffeting him—Fred kept what he thought was a stiff upper lip and an eye to the future.

With Adele out of sight, there was no one to moan to now. Fred knew better than to moan too much to Phyllis. She might tire of his self-castigation and agonies. He was worried—damned worried. He might be out of show business entirely if he was unable to get himself a big hit.

Still, there was always that remote possibility of . . . Hollywood. He hated to think about what a change of mediums would mean, but there it was. *If* he could make it. And that was certainly an unknown quality.

It was time to find out if he really *could* make the switch; if he could not, he would work something else out. At least he had *The Gay Divorce* to continue with. The London version of the show would open in the fall of 1933. That took care of his professional future for a while.

It embittered him that the screen test he had made with Adele in 1928 had been a plus for Adele and such a minus for him. Whatever the details of the verdict on the test had been, there was no question but that the Astaires had failed to land a contract on the strength of it.

In effect, he had been rejected once—resoundingly. But Fred's whole life had been a long series of ups and downs. He had failed before, only to come back a week later and succeed—to be followed by another flop. That was simply the nature of the theatrical beast that he rode.

Quietly he put out feelers to Hollywood. It was in his mind that *The Gay Divorce* was more or less *he*. If he could sell the entire property to the movies, he could go along with it. In his initial discussions, it was an Astaire–*The Gay Divorce* package that he tried to merchandise.

Eddie McIlvaine was an agent who at the time was associated with Leland Hayward. Through McIlvaine, Hayward got the word and became Fred's conduit to Hollywood. One of Hayward's closest friends in the movie industry was producer David O. Selznick. Selznick had a habit of bouncing around from one studio to another. He was then in his RKO period.

Although musical comedies had been going through a very bad period in 1930 and 1931—possibly because of the onset of the Great Depression—there was sudden revived interest in the big money being earned by Maurice Chevalier and Jeanette MacDonald in *Love Me Tonight* (Paramount) and Eddie Cantor in *The Kid from Spain*, (M-G-M), two smash musicals that had surprised everyone in 1932.

The Hayward-Selznick conversation resulted in these memoed thoughts from Selznick:

> I am tremendously enthused about the suggestion [obviously made by Leland Hayward] of using Fred Astaire. If he photographs . . . he may prove to be a really sensational bet. . . . Astaire is one of the greatest artists of the day: a magnificent performer, a man conceded to be perhaps, next to Leslie Howard, the most charming in the American theater, and unquestionably the outstanding young leader of American musical comedy.

There was no mention of *The Gay Divorce* in the memo. Perhaps Selznick had taken only part of Hayward's proposal to heart.

Merian C. Cooper, then one of Selznicks' producers at RKO, agreed with Selznick. He had seen *The Band Wagon* in New York and had been particularly impressed with Fred's abilities. He conceded that Astaire was "a hell of a dancer" and added that "there wasn't anybody in his class."

The upshot of all this was a telephone call from Selznick to Hayward requesting a screen test of Fred Astaire. Hayward and Astaire made the test in January 1933 in a New York studio, and the film was sent out to the Coast immediately.

When the front-office brass at RKO took a look at the test, there was a noticeable chilling of the atmosphere in the screening room. Selznick, who was still pushing for Astaire, retreated a bit in his thinking. Another memo resulted, of which the following is a part:

"I am a little uncertain about the man, but I feel, in spite of his enormous ears and bad chin line, that his charm is so tremendous that it comes through even in this wretched test."

Others were not so sanguine, but Selznick was running things, and he had the final say. Like Abraham Lincoln when faced with a similar situation with his recalcitrant cabinet during the Civil War: "Seven nays, one aye. Gentlemen, the ayes have it."

But Selznick's reluctance was transmuted to wild enthusiasm on the other end of the transcontinental telephone wire. Hayward dropped by the theater that same night to tell Astaire: "Fred, you're a cinch. I was talking to David Selznick on the long-distance phone today. He's head of RKO. They want you for a big musical, *Flying Down to Rio*, when you're through here."

Fred nodded, wondering what had happened to *The Gay Divorce*, although he said nothing about it. Hollywood might come through later with the Cole Porter musical. He wondered what *Flying Down to Rio* was all about. It sounded like an outdoor adventure film of some kind.

In retrospect, it seems doubtful that even with the known persuasive powers of Hayward and Selznick a contract could have been executed between RKO and Fred Astaire had it not been for the unexpected success of yet another musical—this one produced by Darryl F. Zanuck in one of his earlier incarnations as producer at Warner Brothers—a picture choreographed by Busby Berkeley. The picture was *42nd Street*, a title that even today reverberates with nostalgia on Broadway.

That musical was cleaning up. Oddly enough, one member of the cast was an old friend of Fred's and now a Hollywood actress— Ginger Rogers. She played a girl called Anytime Annie, with the gag line "The only time Anytime Annie said no, she didn't hear the question!" In the film she worked with Una Merkel in the famed "Shuffle off to Buffalo" number.

In the midst of all this excitement and indecision, David O. Selznick suddenly packed up and left RKO to go to work for his father-in-law, Louis B. Mayer, at M-G-M. That left a huge vacuum at financially troubled RKO. The question again came up. Musicals were *in*. Who to get for *Flying Down to Rio*? Even Selznick had had his reservations about Astaire. Should they go for him or try someone else?

One of the young directors who wanted to make a name for himself at RKO was Mark Sandrich; he thought his future lay in musicals. He was anxious to work with Astaire and had faith in him in spite of the tests. Sandrich began a campaign with Merian C. Cooper—now suddenly in charge of production at RKO in Selznick's absence—to convert Lou Brock to Astaire. Brock was the designated producer of *Rio*—hell, he had written the original story!—and he might be able to call the turns on Astaire so Sandrich could have a shot at him in the future.

And Brock *needed* a dancer to cast in his brainchild. In the chaos left by the departure of Selznick, Brock got the okay from Cooper to sign on Astaire. He did the negotiating. Hayward was no fool, and he was representing Astaire. Between the two of them it was verbally agreed that Astaire would be assigned the lead in the movie. Fred knew that a Broadway star transplanted to Hollywood would get absolutely *nothing* if he were submerged in some song-and-dance bit part. It had to be the lead or nothing. Opposite him the studio planned to star Helen Broderick, who had appeared with Astaire on Broadway in *The Band Wagon*.

It was at this juncture, with the *Rio* script by Anne Caldwell, based on Lou Brock's original story, now being rewritten for Astaire, that the contracts were signed between RKO and Fred. He would enter motion pictures as a star, and he would thus be guaranteed a certain amount of control over the filming and cutting of his numbers. Nothing less than top status would give him that right. He did not want to wind up as one of twelve million dancing partners in a Busby Berkeley spectacular.

On May 27, 1933, the contracts were signed. Astaire was to begin work on August 1, 1933, in *Flying Down to Rio*. The contract stipulated that he would be paid $1,500 a week for his work in the film. He had already agreed to go to London with *The Gay Divorce* in the fall of 1933, and so RKO would shoot *Rio* in the summer, after the New York run of *Divorce* was over. The contract also said that the studio would take out an option on a second film; if that option was to be exercised, Fred would make $1,750 a week on the second film and $2,000 on the third. And so on.

Everything looked very rosy for the future.

Fred called up Phyllis and asked her to marry him.

"Oh, not yet!" Phyllis protested. She explained that the future of her son was still in the hands of the courts. She would have to wait until something was decided. Should she marry, she felt that the courts might be tempted to award Peter to his father.

Fred tried not to appear despondent, although he was. He had a solution. "I'll go out there and make the first picture. Then I'll come straight back here afterward. Then we'll be married."

But Phyllis spotted a fallacy. "That's no good. If you go away from me to Hollywood, you'll start running round with some of those girls out there. Whether you do or not, I'd always think you did. We'd better get married right now, as soon as possible."

FADE OUT. In the end, two separate events decided the issue.

One was the action of the divorce court, awarding the custody of Peter to Phyllis on July 10.

The other was that David O. Selznick was "borrowing" Fred from RKO *before* the first days of his contract. Selznick wanted him for a bit part in an M-G-M picture that starred Clark Gable, Franchot Tone, and Joan Crawford. M-G-M would pay his air flight out to Los Angeles in the middle of July to begin shooting.

Thus the marriage of Fred Astaire and Phyllis Livingston Potter took place two days after the court action, on July 12, 1933, with Justice Selah B. Strong performing the ceremony in his chambers in Brooklyn, New York.

The Astaires had a one-day honeymoon, which they spent cruising the Hudson River on Mrs. Payne Whitney's yacht, the *Captiva*, by themselves.

On the very next day the Astaires boarded a Transcontinental-Western Air Ford trimotor plane for California. "Transcontinental-Western Air" was the original merger that formed TWA, later renamed Trans-World Airlines. This was in 1933, and it took them "twenty-six hours, I think," as Fred recalled, to get from the East Coast to the West Coast. But they got there, landing at the Burbank Airport in the San Fernando Valley.

They were met dutifully by a studio flack from RKO named Andy Hervey, who had a couple of free-lance photographers with him to take pictures of the newlyweds as they stepped off the plane.

These pictures were published the next day, with the heading "Astaire and Bride Here from East." And the usual Hollywood-oriented material followed, welcoming the Astaires to "Hollywood's motion-picture colony." To the press it was a "colony" then, not an industry or even a proper business.

Within hours the newlyweds were settled in at the Beverly Wilshire Hotel, located at the foot of Rodeo Drive, now the worldwide center of style, opulence, and glamour for shoppers but then just another street filled with shops for the denizens of the movie business.

There Fred tried to figure out the pluses and minuses of this quick guest appearance in the Joan Crawford–Clark Gable picture *Dancing Lady* before shooting the one he was scheduled to debut in at RKO.

To have RKO, the studio that had signed him, lend him out so quickly—and for a bit part!—did not augur well for his staying power at RKO, or for his future in the motion-picture business, for that matter. There was good reason for Moaning Minnie to start in on his act. He began to.

Had Fred Astaire known what associate producer Johnny Considine at M-G-M had said about him after viewing his screen test, he would have been even less certain about his future in films:

"You can get dancers like this for seventy-five dollars a week."

Nor was he yet aware of what had been happening with the property called *Flying Down to Rio*. The lavish scheme of Astaire as leading man with Helen Broderick as costar had changed dramatically when she was found unavailable. A second lead, a Brazilian actor named Raul Roulien, was added to the cast to play against Fred in a plot triangle. Filling out the cast list at that time were Chick Chandler and Arline Judge. A month later, the cast was expanded by the addition of Joel McCrea and Dorothy Jordan.

To take Broderick's place, Dolores Del Rio was signed. When McCrea strayed, Gene Raymond—a platinum blond *male* star— was added. Chandler and Judge vanished, too.

By now the story was canted around to become a vehicle for Dolores Del Rio, not Fred Astaire. Astaire's role was now downgraded to half a dancing team, the other half being Jordan. But that pairing off suddenly came apart when Jordan decided to marry Merian Cooper, the top man at the studio. The two were off on a honeymoon to Europe.

From lead role to part-time dancer in a short six weeks. That was Fred Astaire's fate. But, of course, he had been through it before. It was simply show business!

Besides that, he knew nothing about all this infighting at the studio. He was enjoying his honeymoon!

PART TWO

The Austerlitz-McMath Connection
1933–39

Chapter Seven

State of the Art: The Hollywood Musical

By the early 1930s that changeling offspring of the theater—the motion picture—had grown into a giant that was almost now as big as its theatrical parent. The advent of sound, at first viewed simply as an added feature to underline the miming of voiceless principals—the theory, indeed, of stage melodrama—was now beginning to add a brand-new dimension to the new medium: the thrill of the spoken word.

Now musical comedy, that popular genre of the theater that had hitherto been banned from films because of the lack of sound, was adding new luster to the movies and attracting audiences never before interested in the flickering medium.

Not that the musical was entirely neglected in 1920s films. The very first breakthrough "sound" picture, 1927's *The Jazz Singer*, was certainly a musical in every sense of the word, even if it did not feature big production numbers, dances, and other show-biz elements. In fact, it was musical comedy that soon became *the* brand-new subgenre of the film industry, inspired by the technological changes in the ability of film to carry sound. *The Broadway Melody* (1929) was M-G-M's contribution to the new screen format, as was Paramount's *The Love Parade* (1929). These more or less set the tone for the upcoming genre, along with adaptations of Broadway operettas such as Paramount's 1932 *Love Me Tonight* and M-G-M's 1934 *Merry Widow*. In spite of the success of these musical comedies and operettas, it was obvious that most filmmakers were wedded to the tradition of the "backstage musical," that the only way to introduce songs and dances into a story was in the contextual framework of a big stage show.

The popularity of this type of drama led to new and varied attempts to integrate songs and showgirls into film stories, with the result that finally the studios threw up their hands and strung together a lot of acts in vaudeville fashion to produce *Hollywood*

Revue of 1929 at M-G-M, *King of Jazz* (1930) at Universal, and *Paramount on Parade* (1930).

In 1930 a new facet was added to the genre with *Good News* (M-G-M), a musical set on a college campus. It was no secret to the men who counted the money in the box offices that the college set supported film more than any other segment of society. In a way, this discovery and Hollywood's reaction to it foreshadowed the later proliferation of "beach epics" and "pectorial pix" in the 1960s and 1970s.

During the thirties the different variations of musicals had sorted themselves out into four specific types: the backstage drama, the transplanted operetta, the film revue, and the campus musical. In all these subgenres, however, the keystone for success with the public seemed to be "bigness," "colossality," "grandeur." The more people on the film frame, the rationale went, the bigger the take at the box office.

The contest began in 1930 at Goldwyn-United Artists, with Busby Berkeley's appointment as dance director for *Whoopee*, starring an old vaudeville and Broadway hand, Eddie Cantor. Even some of the regulation operettas like *The Smiling Lieutenant* (Paramount) in 1931 and *One Hour with You* (Paramount) in 1930 began to feature increasing numbers of dancers and extras on the screen.

The Great Depression was beginning finally to affect all areas of show business, and the studios knew that they must churn out lavish spectacle and glamour to try to cheer up the stricken populace. Nevertheless, in spite of adherence to the formula, there was a noticeable falling off of receipts in 1931 and 1932, and most studios began swapping these biggies for cheaper gangster and western epics. Less people, less cost.

Until, of course—as has been previously mentioned—*Love Me Tonight*, *The Kid from Spain*, and *42nd Street*. Now "big—or bust" was the prescribed formula for the success or failure of the musical. In spite of this, most of the studios had turned out musicals during that early period, including RKO, which had signed up Fred Astaire for *Flying Down to Rio*. RKO was not one of the strong Hollywood movie studios. It had always fluttered somewhere between complete disaster and financial depletion. It seemed always to be in need of mouth-to-mouth resuscitation, usually in the form of greenbacks.

Its thirteen acres on the northeast corner of Gower and Melrose had been originally a part of Hollywood Cemetery—hardly an auspicious beginning for a firm in an industry steeped in mysticism, superstition, and the reading of tea leaves, entrails, and "signs." The company was then called Film Booking Offices—

FBO—even though it was incorporated as Robertson-Cole Productions. From 1921 to 1926 the company simply floundered along, unable to get anything going of any note. It was known for its "usual melodramas," in the telling words of movie historian Daniel Blum.

Joseph P. Kennedy, at that time not really having decided whether to be a maker of whoopie, a maker of movies, or a maker of presidents, became interested in a top silent screen star named Gloria Swanson. She had begun as a Mack Sennett bathing beauty. Kennedy wanted to further her career, which was at its peak in the mid-twenties. Actually it was *his* career he was thinking about. He wanted her to star in pictures for *him*. He had some money, but not a fortune. He decided to concentrate on the West Coast instead of Wall Street for a short while and purchased floundering FBO in 1926.

He continued to try to woo her to FBO, but when Swanson left Paramount, she went instead to United Artists and not to Kennedy's thirteen acres of gravesite. The studio was in constant trouble during the Kennedy years, making such thrillers as *Red Hot Hoofs*, with Tom Tyler, *One Number to Play*, with Red Grange and May McAllen, *Tarzan and the Golden Lion*, with James Pierce and Edna Murphy, along with comedies like *Clancy's Kosher Wedding*, with Rex Lease and Shawn Lynn (an obvious rip-off of Broadway's *Abie's Irish Rose*) and musical college films like *Her Summer Hero*, with Sally Blane, Harold Goodwin, Clive Moore, and Duane Thompson.

In a Wall Street manipulation that became a textbook assault, Kennedy gained secret control of the Keith-Albee-Orpheum stocks. He then ousted the owners and merged the huge theater chain into FBO, renaming it Radio- (for Sarnoff's Radio Corporation of America) Keith-Orpheum (for the vaudeville chain). Thus, RKO. Since the initials meant little, the logo it developed—a radio tower with sparks flying out of the top—contained the words "RKO Radio Pictures" despite the redundancy.

By that time, Kennedy was becoming enamored once again of Wall Street financing and turned his attention to the stock market. Later he would become head of the Securities and Exchange Commission (SEC). And he had a number of sons.

On Kennedy's departure, the studio was in the charge of William LeBaron, with whom the Astaires had worked on Broadway in *Apple Blossoms* and for which LeBaron had written the book and lyrics; he also wrote the ill-fated *Love Letter* in which the Astaires had flopped.

Under LeBaron the studio produced several musicals, one of them *Rio Rita*, a Flo Ziegfeld 1927 stage hit on Broadway. Critics agreed that it was "the most successful movie adaptation of a musical comedy . . . to date." It was an opulent production, with the last half of the film shot in Technicolor. This was *before* the stock-market crash. John Boles and Bebe Daniels starred, with the comedy team of Bert Wheeler and Robert Woolsey backing them up in their film debut. The plot of this concerned the unmasking of a personable bandit chief: Was he indeed Rio Rita's brother?

LeBaron also made *The Vagabond Lover* in 1929, featuring Rudy Vallee in a simpy story about a saxophone player who infiltrates into a Long Island mansion by impersonating the man who taught him how to play the sax. How's that again? Marie Dressler, as the nouveau riche society matron, was by far the best feature of this sagging effort.

Better was the later production of *Dixiana*, starring Bebe Daniels again and Everett Marshall, late of the Metropolitan Opera. Wheeler and Woolsey supplied some gags, but the main attraction was the superior performance of the great black tap dancer Bill Robinson doing a production number featuring some of his most intricate steps.

Within four years, LeBaron was replaced by David O. Selznick. In spite of the real ingenuity in presenting Bill Robinson in a dance sequence, the studio was in deep financial straits. Selznick brought in new actors and new properties. Ann Harding, Leslie Howard, and Myrna Loy made *The Animal Kingdon* in 1932. *King Kong* was a technological thriller done with consummate skill by Merian Cooper, Selznick's second-in-command, hired from Paramount. Selznick brought in Katharine Hepburn, fresh from her New York stage success in *Holiday*, to do *A Bill of Divorcement* as her movie debut. Constance Bennett was hired to make *What Price Hollywood*. Hepburn later made *Little Women*.

And it was of course Selznick who had set the wheels in motion for the hiring of Fred Astaire, even though he had not actually been in charge when the papers were signed. In fact, Selznick was not sure if any papers had been signed at RKO or not—or how they were worded if they had been.

Dancing Lady was a vehicle created especially for Joan Crawford in an attempt by Louis B. Mayer to cast her in a quality picture after two fiascos in a row. The contribution by Fred Astaire to this "musical" was minute, to put it gently. It consisted of three tiny bits: a brief rehearsal routine and two hunks of eye-catching singing and dancing in an onstage production number at the end of the picture.

In the original bit, Fred appears as himself—Fred Astaire, a professional dancer—to rehearse with Crawford. Gable calls him over and introduces him. He starts the dance with her, and almost immediately Crawford pulls a ligament or something and falls to the floor. Exit Fred. The story follows Crawford, of course.

Later on, Fred's first bit in the production number is an obvious rip-off of "I Love Louisa," from his show *The Band Wagon*. Called "Let's Go Bavarian," it features Astaire dancing in an obvious cutesy-pie costume, going through the motions with plenty of broad hand gestures. A second segment, "High-Ho the Gang's All Here," shows him in white tie and tails, dancing with a whole raft of people. No solos—but he *seems* to be having a good time.

One thing is notable in his debut appearance on film. He instinctively did all he could in dancing with Crawford to adapt to her limitations and strengths in dancing, and in the end he makes her look good—better, indeed, than she would have looked in anyone else's hands, or actually arms.

Fred later said:

> There have been stories to the effect that I was buried in that picture, that no one on the lot appreciated me, that I was treated as an ugly duckling, and that Miss Crawford's company overlooked an opportunity to sign me up.
>
> They may be interesting stories, but they aren't true. I was under contract to another company and was merely borrowed for *Dancing Lady*. The script called for a dance, and I danced it; several executives said I was good and that they wished I could stay on the lot; and after I finished the job I returned to the home studio, a more practiced motion-picture actor than I was when I left it. . . . As a result, I did a much better job in *Rio* than would have been possible if it had been my first picture."

In fact, when *Dancing Lady* was previewed, he was singled out for favorable notice by several reviewers. "I was pleased with lots of things but kept thinking of what I would like to try if I ever got in a position to make my own decisions."

When Fred Astaire finally learned of the shambles at RKO with *Flying Down to Rio*, he almost threw up his hands in despair. As yet no one had been assigned to be his dancing partner, at least to Fred's knowledge. From star of the picture he was now down in fifth position on the cast list.

It was always Fred's habit to turn that grim period into a joke, as witness this recollection in a later interview:

> Since I was going to make a picture, I wanted to be an actor who danced, not just another dancer, and soon after I arrived in Hollywood, I visted the producer's office and

began the conversation, "I have been dancing for more than twenty years, and—"

"Well," he said. "Sit down. You must be tired!"

It was such a good gag I forget what I had come in to say.

The truth of the matter was otherwise. At this point, Fred did indeed begin talking to Lou Brock, the producer of the picture, and Merian Cooper, the head of the studio. He talked about *The Gay Divorce*, which was the package—bound up with him in it—that he had originally proposed for his Hollywood debut. This discussion got him nowhere. It was a matter of money. *Rio* was already in the house. *Divorce* would have cost big money.

Finally, three days after Fred had settled in at RKO, he was told who his dancing partner was to be. It was his old acquaintance Ginger Rogers!

"I selected Ginger Rogers—at that time not a big name—as Astaire's partner," Cooper recalled years later.

Originally I was going to use my wife [Dorothy Jordan] to play opposite him, but our marriage made me revise that plan. While the numbers were in rehearsal, I brought in Robert Benchley to write some additional dialogue for Astaire, and in other ways we built up the parts of Astaire and Rogers.

Some, but not really all that much.

The Ginger whom Fred now saw was quite different from the Ginger he had choreographed and squired around in New York. She had become a veteran screen actress of some twenty-odd pictures, although some of the parts had been quite small. On Broadway, she was a redheaded girl who could dance reasonably well and sing and say a few lines. Once in Hollywood, she had changed her image when Jean Harlow came in, tinting her red hair blond and turning into the typical 1920s gold digger—another Joan Blondell, so to speak. That was the Ginger that Fred now saw sitting opposite him at RKO—a little coarse, a little brash, but with a kind of pleasant vulnerability in spite of the hard shell.

FRED: Do you like this picture?

GINGER: I don't know. Do you?

FRED: I'm a stranger. I don't know anything. But I like it here.

GINGER: Well, to tell you the truth, I didn't want to do any musicals. I was satisfied to keep on with the straight ones. But I guess it'll turn out all right. Anyway, we'll have some fun.

And they did.

Flying Down to Rio concerned a triangle involving a Latin lady, a Latin man, and an *Americano*. The American is Gene Raymond, a band leader, his accordionist-singer-dancer is Fred Astaire, "Fred Ayres" (get it?), and his featured singer is Ginger Rogers, "Honey Hale."

In view of the Astaire-Rogers team and its long string of hits in the next seven years, it is interesting to see that they were apart more than together in this initial offering. Ginger does the song "Music Makes Me," which was later used as the background for a solo tap for Fred; Fred sings "Flying Down to Rio" together with a chorus; "Orchids in the Moonlight" is a dance in which Fred works with Dolores Del Rio. Only in "The Carioca" do Fred and Ginger dance together.

The plot concerns Raymond's love for Del Rio; he chases her all the way to Rio de Janeiro to make love to her—hence the song title "Flying Down to Rio." Of course, he has arranged a booking for his band to pay for the time. Once in Rio, the band scouts out the local talent, and it is at the Carioca Casino that the big production number, "The Carioca," occurs.

The central gimmick of this dance, a fast tango, written with panache by Vincent Youmans, is the forehead-to-forehead touching of the partners while each does a complete turn without breaking contact. Dave Gould, the dance director, was auditioning a young hopeful for assistant director when the candidate, Hermes Pan, suggested doing what the lyrics say to do: "Two heads together / They say / Are better than one / Two heads together / That's how / The dance is begun." He demonstrated what he meant to Gould and got the job.

Later, Pan met with Fred when Fred was rehearsing one of his routines. Pan knew all about Fred's methods and his perfectionism— thus, he was diffident about offering any suggestions. It soon developed that Fred was searching for a step to bridge a sticky part of the routine. Quite soon Pan came up with a suggestion that Fred liked; he used it in the film. It gave Pan confidence and helped get him started in his long career in films. A lifelong friendship began between him and Astaire, one that lasted all through Astaire's last film, *Finian's Rainbow*.

The Astaire-Rogers dancing combination in "The Carioca" only made it through two of the many segments of the production number. Gould was doing a Busby Berkeley here, with dozens of dancers and singers. In the very first dance sequence for Astaire, he manages a deft little tap-and-ballroom combination: a tap warmup, a demonstration of the Carioca pose with the band, a quick lift, a coordinated spin, and a development of the Carioca idea as the dancers whirl around, keeping their heads together. There are some fast ballroom spins, some complex tap phrases, in which Fred and Ginger do a kind of Fred-and-Adele duel, and some more shoulder shimmying, including Fred's old trick of fluttering his hands. The two dancers then bump heads comically, stagger around, and the camera cuts away.

The rest is a clutter of swaying dancers, singers, and revelers. A black woman sings the song; blacks fill the dance floor. For nineteen seconds Astaire and Rogers return to do a hot Carioca tap on top of seven revolving white-painted pianos. In all, the new team dances only a bare two minutes together in the entire movie!

Later, when Roulien and Del Rio are involved in the lush treatment of "Orchids in the Moonlight," Raymond shows up. A confrontation is in the works. Fred dances off with Del Rio to neutralize an embarrassing situation.

The next day, Astaire is rehearsing a quartet of girl singers when Raymond leads the band in "Music Makes Me." This is an Astaire gimmick dance; he finds the music takes over his body completely, without his willing it, and he does a gag number, playing it as if impelled to against his will. It is a spiffy, athletic, fast-paced, and ingenious tap dance, obviously that of an expert. At the end of fifty seconds, the music stops, and Fred simply goes on with his conversation with the quartet as if nothing had happened. What a tease it was for the audience!

When Fred saw the rushes—the scenes shot during the day—he was appalled. "When *Rio* was finished," he confessed later, "I wished I could burn all the film."

Although Marie Dressler had warned me and told me she always felt dreadful for days after she saw herself on the screen and Maurice Chevalier said it would be a terrific shock, I wasn't prepared for the very peculiar Fred Astaire who appeared before me on the screen. Friends tried to comfort me by promising that I wouldn't look so bad to audiences, but I was sure my first guess had been right. This was the end of my moving-picture career.

He once said that he thought he "was a weird-looking character, anyway. I never liked the way I photographed particularly." In his eyes, his dancing seemed ponderous, his bony American face bizarre on the screen. He found Pandro Berman, one of the head producers at RKO, and begged him either to remake or delete his numbers. "I'll do them over free," he told Berman.

When Berman turned him down, telling him, "Don't be silly. Everybody likes it. You've got a great chance."

He didn't believe it and went around to everyone he had met in town thanking them for being so nice to him while he was there.

The Astaires had leased a house on North Cañon Drive for six months, and at the end of Fred's stint at RKO, they packed up for London, where Fred was due to open in the English run of *The Gay Divorce*. Some days after that the Astaires picked up Peter in New York, where he was attending school, and sailed for England.

Convinced that he was through in films before he ever began, Moaning Minnie opened in London with Claire Luce on November 3, 1933. The show went well—all except the finale—the over-the-furniture romp. During the most energetic part of it, Claire tripped and sent both of them sprawling. Although she was able to continue, she was in obvious pain. She hung in through the show's run but afterward was forced to spend a lengthy stay in the hospital. It was discovered that she had damaged her hip badly in the fall. Indeed, the fall actually put an end to her dancing career. She went on to score as playwright-actress in *The Women*.

Nor was Claire Luce the only one who suffered that season. Adele had given birth to a baby girl prematurely. When the girl died, Adele remained ill for weeks. Finally, she did get to see the show with Fred in it.

"I think I danced well every night except the one when Adele came to see the show," Fred said. "It was the first time she ever sat in the audience and watched me dance. To see her out in front instead of beside me threw me all out of balance. I was self-conscious and felt that I was giving a bad performance."

Bad? Adele thought otherwise.

"I'd never seen him from out front before," she said. "It was also the first time I realized that Fred had sex appeal. Fred. Wherever did he get it?"

An English play reviewer got the same impression. James Agate suggested that Astaire's secret on the stage was indeed sex—"sex bejewelled and be-glamoured and be-pixied."

Meanwhile, back in Hollywood the technicians and directors were beginning to assemble the scraps of film they had taken in the summer to see what they had in *Flying Down to Rio*—a turkey or a bonanza.

Chapter Eight

A Marriage of Convenience

From the beginning, the "marriage" of Fred Astaire and RKO Radio Pictures was a chancy, tentative thing. Neither actually held out much hope for a longtime alliance. Fred, then at the peak of his art, should certainly have been desirous of tying up with a motion-picture production company in a somewhat better financial position—if only, through its prestige and clout, to enhance his own emerging image.

Because of RKO's inability to sign performers of the first order, it was constantly forced to settle for second best—second best or up-and-coming stars and cinema professionals and technicians anxious to get a start in this most competitive of industries.

Astaire was bringing three distinct talents to this odd marriage: his formidable ability to dance and to choreograph; his very underrated talent for singing and *selling* songs; and his still growing ability to speak lines and act on a comic-dramatic level. These were indeed remarkable pluses. In the minus column was his appearance, as evidenced by his screen tests, and the unknown quality of his appeal to movie audiences that were required to pay money to see him.

RKO's negatives had been mentioned. So have several of its positives: especially its freewheeling proclivity for taking a chance, its inventiveness, and its genius at innovation. With these, the studio brought along several more positive elements, as well. Chief among them, of especial importance to the eventual success of Astaire as a film dancer, was technical acumen in cinematography and set design.

It must not be forgotten that it is the setting of any jewel that showcases its essential beauty, that makes it sparkle and shine. At RKO it was the art department that must be given credit for providing the rich and lush backgrounds that enabled the dances of Fred Astaire to scintillate so brilliantly.

That these years with Ginger Rogers were to be known as "the golden years" for Astaire owes much to the wild and woolly no-holds-barred Art Deco flair of the set designs that illuminated every one of their pictures. Most portraits and retrospectives of Astaire are now enhanced with Art Deco graphics, as if he were a part of the movement. The fact is that of course Astaire and Rogers were always backed up—shown off—by the gleaming, streamlined, modern lines of the sets that were a part of the RKO neoclassic mystique.

In his definitive book *Designing Dreams*, Donald Albrecht explores the concept of modern architecture by studying its influence in movies from their beginnings to modern times. In the section on Hollywood in the thirties, he concentrates on the "moderne" design concept as it was evoked by three studios—Paramount, RKO, and M-G-M. M-G-M's sets were lavish, modern, and well executed, with plenty of Academy Awards going to its art directors. Paramount's sets were influenced by the German designs of Richard Neutra, Walter Gropius, and Mies van der Rohe.

RKO's were somewhat different from these two, a result of the studio's constant struggle with poverty and its inevitable need to innovate to save money. "Designers at RKO Studios invented their own fanciful and decorative amalgams of modern architecture, streamlined Art Deco, and neo-classicism" is the way he puts it.

This style, he goes on, is most consistently seen in the eight Astaire-Rogers movies the studio made between 1933 and 1939. The art director in charge of the sets during these years was Van Nest Polglase, who had started in movies with Famous Players-Lasky in 1919. He had then worked briefly for M-G-M and Paramount. There, at Paramount, according to Albrecht, "he reputedly introduced the notion of the 'all-white' set."

Shortly afterward, in 1932, Selznick hired Polglase at RKO, the year before *Rio* went in front of the cameras. Polglase's chief assistant, or unit art director, on this movie and on the future Astaire-Rogers movies was Carroll Clark. The chief set designer was Allan Abbott. The art department itself consisted of an ever shifting, changing group of men.

Among the most consistent, and working on all eight of the pictures cited, was Robert M. Cassiday, a California architect who had worked in Los Angeles and on the Honolulu City Hall job just before the Depression hit, when he was unable to find work in a housing market totally depleted by the failing economy. He hired on at RKO as one of the architectural designers whose responsibility it was to produce working drawings for the carpenters who had to put these streamlined sets together.

Cassiday once recalled:

The dance floor surfaces became a problem when Astaire joined the studio and finally evolved his own concept of the dance. The idea was to see him and his partner glide effortlessly across vast expanses of gleaming smoothness—a dream world. For that soft, sensuous surface we used ordinary flooring covered with bakelite or formica and sometimes even vitrolite, which gave it a gleaming black gloss. This was no problem with *Rio*, of course. Except for a brief tap dance on a regular dance-floor surface, most of Astaire's part in the Carioca was danced on the top of seven white pianos.

The set for "The Carioca" number was about the only big one Polglase was in personal charge of during his tenure at RKO. As his responsibilities grew, he became an executive head who handed out assignments to others.

Van dreamed up the swirls and the decor of the *Rio* set. The rest of us had to figure out how to build the darned thing. The concept of his "white set" was a natural for the "Carioca Casino," which was its script name. Since it was an outdoor casino, the idea of sunshine, light, *and* space seemed right. And so Van turned on white full blast.

A look at that set now, with its twin curving stairs, the seven white pianos in the middle, the high concave walls etched lightly with sketchy murals, and the giant butterflies high on the parapets, gives one a sense of delight and freedom—the whole idea of the dance that was calculated to take the minds of Depression-wearied America off its troubles.

"The color white was a secret weapon we didn't even know we had when Astaire came to us," Cassiday pointed out.

"Most of us Californians had never heard of him. We had no idea that his costume was consistently formal black with gleaming white to set it off. As a matter of fact, in much of *Rio*, Astaire appeared in a light gray suit. None of us even *thought* about him in terms of black and white."

It was also a matter of luck that within the immediate past Eastman Kodak had made some giant technological strides that allowed movie studios to use white in their sets. In the 1920s, white caused such a glare on the screen that it blinded the audience and overwhelmed the actors. Walls had to be painted pastel pink or green to photograph white.

By 1933, J. Roy Hunt and David Abel at RKO had learned how to exploit maximum contrasts in black-and-white photography to evoke a rich, lush effect on the screen. Good white gleamed silver on a good screen, giving the projected picture a real bounce. It was this contrasty technique that Polglase was after, and it was what his art department gave him.

Cassiday said:

> In the "Orchids in the Moonlight" set you can see the neoclassic style of the time. The dance floor is composed of black-and-white chessboard squares; there's a curving stairway with narrow steps and chrome strips for handrails; there's even an upstairs dining area painted to look like an airliner— carrying out the "flight" motif of the picture. Corny but effective.

Was there an audible gasp from the crew when Astaire finally grabbed Rogers and started to dance "The Carioca"?

"Nobody on the set guessed that there was anything different in that dance than in any of the others. In fact, most of the effort was put into getting those huge numbers of chorus dancers on and off the set at the right time."

What did Astaire think of the sets he danced in?

> He didn't like them at all. He felt intimidated by the size. If you've ever been on a sound stage, you'll know what I mean. For him, used to fairly cramped dancing areas, our sets looked like the playing field at the Olympic Coliseum. [The Olympic games had just played Los Angeles in 1932, for which the present Los Angeles Coliseum was constructed. A sound stage generally ran at least two hundred feet the long way.] He also didn't like the clutter of the set—all those dancers and the "audience" watching. He was used to a stage spotlight, of course, and being able to *make* the audience look at him. He thought the camera was robbing him of the ability to make the audience look where he wanted them to look.

This comment is borne out by something Fred told an interviewer at about that time concerning the inability of the motion-picture camera to record a dance properly: "The flat surface of the screen robs it of three-dimensional quality."

"*Rio* was a mishmash of a film, really," Cassiday said.

In a way it was kind of a publicity scheme for Merian C. Cooper, the studio head, who was a former World War I pilot in love with aviation. He was on the board of directors of Pan American Airways, which had just opened an air-express service from Miami to South America in 1932. Sikorsky designed the clipper ships used in the film. Any little bit of publicity might help Pan Am, Cooper figured.

Astaire's dance with Dolores Del Rio—to "Orchids in the Moonlight"—was a graceful ballroom exhibition, very brief, very elegant. But something was lost in it. Fred was right in having his doubts about *Rio.*

In fact, no one knew what the studio had in the can until the editors began their work in splicing together the takes into some semblance of dramatic order. The first thing noted was that Fred might not look like much, but he was a pretty fair comedian. Mortin Eustis later wrote in *Theatre Arts Monthly* that Fred was actually concentrating on his *interpretation* of the role—his acting—to get him through, not on his singing or on his dancing.

"It was strictly as an actor, or comedian, that he hoped to romp through the golden gates of movieland, retaining enough compensation on the way out to guarantee more security than the stage could afford when he became too old to dance eight times a week," Eustis put it.

The second thing noted in assembling *Rio* was that Fred could put over a song on film with seeming ease. And the third thing was even more important—actually the crux of the matter.

It was the sudden appeal of the two dancers—Fred and his partner Ginger Rogers—that made "The Carioca" number sparkle. The production itself was good, almost as good as a Busby Berkeley. But when the camera quite simply focused on Astaire and Rogers, something else came through.

How? Accident? Chemistry? Genius?

To Fred's sophisticated, slightly vulnerable, appealing male, Roger's lissome, easygoing, *friendly* female was, in show-business terms, the spark that set off the dynamite. In fact, a film shot taken almost at random, showing Rogers and Astaire looking up into the sky, was resurrected and made the closeout shot of the film—the idea being subliminally to implant in the audience the idea more next week.

DISSOLVE OUT. DISSOLVE IN . . .

In his autobiography, Astaire playfully passed over those weeks in London before his work at RKO and the opening of *Flying Down to Rio.* "Being so busy with the activities at hand, I complete forgot about the movie situation for a few weeks."

Not so! He was fretting every moment he could set aside to fret. There was no word—no word!—from Hollywood. Why not? He had crashed and burned, that was it. He was out. O-U-T.

When the mail came, he refused to open it. When the phone rang, he wouldn't answer it. Moaning Minnie was in full cry.

A cable arrived that Fred found difficult to open. It was from Pandro S. Berman, now in charge of RKO.

YOU WERE A SWELL SUCCESS IN PREVIEW FLYING DOWN TO RIO LAST NIGHT.

Shortly after that, Hayward called him and told him that his option had been picked up by RKO.

"Tell them to buy *The Gay Divorce!*" Fred suggested again, hoping that Hayward wouldn't get tired of his constant reference to the property.

This time Hayward surprised him. "I have done so. Berman is on his way to London to see you in the show."

Dancing Lady, with Fred's bit part, opened. He was mentioned in most all the notices. Thornton Delahanty even decried "the niggardly use made of Fred Astaire."

Rose Pelswick, in the *New York Evening Journal*: "The star's dancing partner in the revue sequences is the nimble Fred Astaire who, while he isn't given much to do, acquits himself elegantly in those moments when he does appear."

The *New York Evening Sun*: "The film winds to a big musical show wherein Miss Crawford leads the male choruses and clogs it around with ease and with—of all people—Fred Astaire, who you may be sure is put in his proper place."

Only a few weeks later *Flying Down to Rio* opened at Radio City Music Hall in New York. *Variety* saw it for what it was. It summed up the picture in this glowing fashion:

> The main point of *Flying Down to Rio* is the screen promise of Fred Astaire. . . . He's assuredly a bet after this one, for he's distinctly likeable on the screen, the mike is kind to his voice, and as a dancer he remains in a class by himself. The latter observation will be no news to the profession, which has long admitted that Astaire starts dancing where the others stop hoofing.

Back at the salt mines on Gower and Melrose, euphoria was the order of the day. One studio executive, Benjamin Kahane, wrote up an internal memo, calmly taking credit for the discovery of Astaire:

"Fred Astaire steals picture and think properly handled we have created another new and fresh screen personality."

By now Berman was on his way to London to see Astaire. In

New York he stopped off to take a look at the Broadway crop of shows and particularly liked *Roberta*, a musical by Jerome Kern. He bought the property immediately for Irene Dunne, paying $65,000 for it, outbidding Paramount and M-G-M in the process. Of course he was thinking of Astaire and Rogers and the potential they had shown in *Rio* as backups for the main plot line.

Berman had been warned by Lou Brock, the producer of *Rio*, that *The Gay Divorce* was a lousy show. As Berman later recalled the conversation, Brock discussed the script in this somewhat cleaned up fashion: "I can blow a better script than that out of my nose."

In London, Berman sat entranced at the lively Astaire and Luce on the stage, thinking finally, "My God, Lou Brock is crazy."

There was no contest in the matter. Berman bought the show for $20,000, low even for those days and less than one-third the cost of *Roberta*. The Hollywood problem with *The Gay Divorce* was its somewhat sleazy theme: There was a fear in movieland that the whole idea of divorce and the messiness of cooking up divorce evidence would discourage the public from coming out to see the film.

"We'll fix it," Berman promised himself. He was beginning to rub his hands mentally, counting the money already. With Astaire and Rogers dancing in the film . . .

As soon as the news of *Rio*'s smash success percolated through the front office at RKO, and with Berman's constant communication from Europe, plans were set in motion to pair off Astaire and Rogers in the next film—which would be *The Gay Divorce*.

News got to Fred in London about this from Hayward. Hayward was happy about the success of his client. Fred was appalled. It wasn't that he didn't want to do *The Gay Divorce*. His original idea had been to ride into Hollywood on the strength of the show.

But—Ginger Rogers? She wasn't *right* for this cool Claire Luce character.

Besides, Fred didn't want to be typed as half a team. He bellyached to Leland Hayward. He had been paired with Adele since birth. Didn't they think he could do the job alone? From London, he poured it all out on paper:

What's all this talk about me being teamed with Ginger Rogers?" I will *not* have it, Leland! I did not go into pictures to be *teamed* with her or anyone else, and if that is the program in mind for me, I will not stand for it. I don't mind making another picture with her, but as for this *team* idea— it's *out*! I've just managed to live down one partnership and I don't want to be bothered with any more. I'd rather not make any more pictures for Radio if I have to be teamed up with one of those movie "queens." . . . This is no flash of temperament on my part, Leland, and does not call for one of your famous bawling-out letters—please understand that. I'm just against the idea—that's all—and feel that if I'm ever to get anywhere on the screen it will be as *one*, not as two."

Berman was young, but he was learning to deal with temperamental stars, and it was he who administered the soothing syrup. The idea was simple enough; he wired Hayward in New York. Astaire was not yet ready to be a star in his own right. He needed more exposure. And he could stand good support. His telegram concluded:

GINGER ROGERS SEEMS TO GO RATHER WELL WITH HIM AND THERE IS NO NEED ASSUME WE WILL BE MAKING PERMANENT TEAM OF THIS PAIR EXCEPT IF WE CAN ALL CLEAN UP LOT OF MONEY BY KEEPING THEM TOGETHER WOULD BE FOOLISH NOT TO.

Well . . .

Berman had a problem. He had a fantastic pairing of people in Fred and Ginger that seemed to work. But he was dealing not only with Fred's temperament but Ginger's, as well. And Ginger's resolve to become a dramatic actress and not just another pretty pair of legs was supported by her mother, Lela. She was fiercely resolved to mow down anyone who stood in the way of her daughter's success.

Years later Berman would recall:

I'll never forget how horrified Fred was when I notified him that Ginger was going to play the part of a titled English lady in *The Gay Divorcée*. . . . There was resistance of this sort from either Fred or Ginger on *every* picture I proposed. They just didn't want to work together. Also, they fought about Ginger's clothes. Whenever Fred came to me to register a complaint about her sometimes appalling taste in gowns, her mother would jump into the fray, and we'd have a Donnybrook.

For Fred, the idea of being "teamed up" again was putting a damper on his desire to return to the Coast. A British film producer wanted to hire him for a picture in England. An upcoming Dietz-Schwartz revue was slated to open in New York; *they* wanted him. The money was equal to what he would get in Hollywood.

He was tempted. He was being wooed aggressively. He toyed with the idea.

"I'm a bit sour on pictures at the moment," he wrote Hayward, "having read several movie magazines that call me a *rival* to Hal LeRoy!!!" This was a reference to the toddler "Baby" LeRoy, who appeared in a number of movies with W. C. Fields; he was a scene stealer and a cuddly kid who seemed to entrance his audiences. Why, few people knew. Certainly not Fred. "Boy—if they're going to start putting me in that class I think I'll stay on the stage where *mere billing and advertisement cannot* make stars. Unless I can do something outstandingly important, I don't think I want to be bothered with movies."

Meanwhile, Astaire had not yet seen himself in *Flying Down to Rio*. When *The Gay Divorce* closed in London, Fred and Phyllis returned to the States and spent a brief time down in Aiken, South Carolina, where Phyllis's family lived. It was in Augusta, Georgia, that the two of them finally saw the picture.

Fred had, naturally, viewed the rushes and had *hated* himself— *and* "The Carioca." When he watched the dance in the theater, he still hated it, but he was intrigued at the intent interest of all those people sitting around him. The dance certainly seemed to be going over. He was stunned. He had been wrong when he had faulted the dance. It still wasn't technically a *good* dance, but the audience was transported.

"If they think that's good," he told himself, "surely I can do something better than that."

It was then and there that he realized something that he had never thought about before. Dancing could be made to project as effectively in black-and-white shadows as in the flesh.

Black and white . . .

It should have been obvious to him, as it was now becoming obvious to others, that he and Rogers—he in his black tails and she in her blond lissomeness—were the perfect match for the black-and-white decor of the Art Deco RKO style. It was a marriage of convenience.

When Fred returned to the West Coast, he was determined to have it out with Merian Cooper. He found instead that Pandro Berman, his main champion, was in charge of the studio. Cooper was still the head man, but he had suffered a heart attack and was recuperating in Hawaii. With Lou Brock on several other pictures, Berman now decided to produce *The Gay Divorce* himself. He hired Mark Sandrich as director. The same dance director was assigned to Astaire again: Dave Gould. His assistant, not to receive any credits, was Hermes Pan, who would work with Astaire and Rogers directly.

About that "team" of Astaire and Rogers . . .

Berman and Astaire went at it head-to-head. In the end, Fred agreed to do the picture with Rogers. But he gained several important concessions from Berman, which will be discussed later. Riding on the success of *Flying Down to Rio*, the set budgets for *The Gay Divorcée* zoomed upward. Berman, incidentally, considered the word "divorce" too harsh for the American public. Anyway, what ever could be "gay" about a divorce? In his mind, he figured that a *divorcée* might be "gay," since finally she would be free from the millstone around her neck. (At the time, of course, the adjective had not assumed its modern homosexual meaning.)

The script was sent out for dry cleaning. Dwight Taylor had appropriated the original plot of an unproduced play entitled *An Adorable Adventure* by J. Hartley Manners, Taylor's stepfather (Laurette's second husband). Taylor's original play had already been retouched and restructured by Samuel Hoffenstein and Kenneth Webb to make it into the musical-comedy libretto of *The Gay Divorce*.

Now this material was given to several more writers to make the story a little less anachronistic—read, old-fashioned. The screenplay that eventually emerged was credited to George Marion, Jr., Dorothy Yost, and Edward Kaufman. As mentioned earlier, the plot concerned the machinations of a "divorce weekend" at a resort.

The original play was set in Brighton, England, a beach resort. In the Broadway musical, the setting was unspecified. By the time the story reached screenplay stage, it took place nowhere—or, rather, a dreamed-up, imaginary place inhabited by well-groomed, well-dressed "swells." In effect, setting and characters were both unrealities, strictly out of the imagination. In a way, it set a style for all the Astaire-Rogers vehicles to come.

In character types and dramatic structure, the show was a prototype. Hero (Fred) and heroine (Ginger) each have confidants: Fred has a bumbling "Uncle Dudley" sidekick in Edward Everett Horton; Ginger has a dithering Alice Brady as hers. The third angle of the triangle—the real live corespondent—is Erik Rhodes, an eyebrow-twitching Latinesque Lothario. And for comedy relief—although *everyone* gets laughs in this effort—there is Eric Blore. Both Rhodes and Blore played in the show's Broadway cast. These character types and their relative positions in the plot structure were to return again and again in the Astaire-Rogers films.

Some laundering was required in the film scenario to placate the newly established Hays Office, a self-policing group then operating in Hollywood to watchdog the movies and expunge any questionable double entendres that might prove objectionable to the moralists.

In the stage musical, when the heroine mistakenly thinks the hero is a hired corespondent, she hands him her room key:

"Here," she says. "Come to my room at ten o'clock. And bring your pajamas."

The Marion/Yost/Kaufman substitute line in the movie is "I'll be waiting for you in my room. Two-sixteen. At midnight."

In fact, the Hays Office suggested that the studio not make the film at all!

The musical score was eviscerated almost completely. The only tune written by Cole Porter that remained was "Night and Day." All the other Porter songs from the original musical were dropped. To fill these vacancies, a number of efforts were added by the team of Harry Revel and Mack Gordon, including "Don't Let It Bother You" and "Let's K-nock K-nees." The big production number, "The Continental," was written by Con Conrad and Herb Magidson; they also wrote one other song, "A Needle in a Haystack."

The key number in the movie was of course "The Continental," and to showcase this brilliantly, the art department supplied the "big white set," or BWS, as it was known. By now, the BWS was not actually all white at all but black and white—a contrasty and exciting combination of opposites.

The Gay Divorcée became the first motion picture whose story line was held together almost exclusively by its dance numbers. The songs were important, as well, and each one of them was carefully integrated into the action of the plot. It will be remembered that it had been Fred's intention to knit "Night and Day" and all the rest of the songs into the Broadway book, as well.

Fred's first solo in the picture is the infectious "A Needle in a Haystack," in which he breaks into a dance as he dresses, thinking about his previous meeting with Ginger Rogers. It is a "getting dressed" routine, with a few interesting ballet cabrioles (jumping up and thrashing the legs in the air) thrown in. The lyrics are sold by Fred's frolicsome verve and bounce.

"Night and Day" is the skillfully reconstituted song and dance from the original musical comedy. The seduction motif is exactly the same, rearranged only slightly to fit the various parameters of the movie setting and to help Astaire's partner do the kind of dancing she did best.

"Ginger was a Charleston dancer when I first met her," Fred said, "and she hadn't had any real experience with dances like 'Night and Day.' By the time we got Ginger into this thing, she just sold it beautifully." An understatement in the familiar Astaire tradition.

Next comes "The Continental," an attempt to manufacture

110

another dance hit like "The Carioca." The production number is divided into three main parts: a duet, a chorus dance, and a closing duet. It is a very long dance by movie standards. A typical dance routine at that time consumed about three minutes on the screen. "The Continental" went on for sixteen minutes! At the end of the dance, Astaire and Rogers do a little tango up a staircase, a czardas at the top, and then a broadly interpreted Viennese waltz back down the stairs again. Then there is some more tap and a dash up the stairs and out the revolving doors.

"The Continental" never made it in the dance halls the way "The Carioca" did, although there were certainly attempts made to whomp it up into a big new dance step.

Nevertheless, the picture was a smash with the public and with the critics alike.

One excerpt should serve to get over the general idea:

> In addition to being a magnificent dancer, Mr. Astaire is an excellent comedian and an engaging leading man. For a second virtue, the photoplay gives the freshly charming Miss Ginger Rogers an opportunity to prove that she is almost as perfect an example of feminine desirability in musical comedy as Miss Myrna Loy is in straight dramatic works. . . . The film has a dash, a polished humor, an air of fresh tunefulness, and a genial charm of playing that makes it one of the most delightful examples of its type of cinema that has ever been devised.

That from Richard Watts.

Fred had done it. He had played out his three talents and made them viable. He had acted, he had sung, and he had, most of all, danced. Throughout the picture he had been the star in total control.

Plus which, he had taken hold of what he considered to be the weakest element of his cinema image—the way his dances were filmed—and had actually *done* something about that. One more step and he would be in complete control of the dances he wanted to create.

Chapter Nine

The Camera Will Dance

The negotiations conducted between Fred Astaire and RKO were, to the ultimate dismay of his agent Leland Hayward, not specifically about money but about artistic control of the dance routines in Fred's movies. In those days it was almost unheard of for a performer, no matter what his or her status, to try to usurp any of the studio's vaunted prerogatives.

But Fred knew what he wanted. He once said, "Either the camera will dance, or I will." What he finally came to demand was the result of what he saw—or, actually, *failed* to see—on the screen, particularly in regard to his own first dances.

To him, a dance was an artistic statement made by the body of a dancer. To be right, it must progress from one moment to the next, in an unbroken flow. The image of the dancer must be seen at all times, in its entirety, *with no visual break.*

Thus, in filmic terms, any dance must be filmed from beginning to end with no breaks—or, at most, a *minimum* of such breaks— cuts, inserts, or moving the camera away from the dancer to feature someone or something else.

In an interview Fred once elaborated on this.

In the old days, they used to cut up all the dances on the screen. In the middle of a sequence, they would show you a close-up of the actor's face, or of his feet, insert trick angles taken from the floor, the ceiling, through lattice work, or a maze of fancy shadows. The result was that the dance had no continuity. The audience was far more conscious of the camera than of the dance. And no matter how effective the trick angles and cockeyed shots might have been in themselves, they destroyed the flow of the dance—a factor which is just as important on the screen as on the stage.

This was what Fred was fighting for—continuity in dance. With the obvious success of *Flying Down to Rio* and the even greater success of *The Gay Divorcée*, he found himself in a position to ask for it—nay, demand it. Of course, the front office was stunned. No one had ever before criticized the studio's technical expertise. That was all arcane mechanical magic. To think that a dancer could want to become his own cameraman. . . .

What was the point, he asked, in keeping the audience apprised of how the dance was being viewed by a fake "audience" at a casino? Why bother? Every time the camera cut away from the dancers, the *real* paying audience in the movie house was being cheated.

It was pointed out to him in some desperation that dancing was tough to photograph and that the cameras had to be planted at various places in order to be able to capture the dance. But indeed, Fred pointed out, the camera could "pan"—he even used the new term he had picked up, which meant the steady movement of a camera sweeping to left or to right to follow an action. The camera was also able to move backward and forward, to a degree. The crane on which the camera was mounted could move almost anywhere it wanted to.

Technically difficult, Fred was told. The background tended to blur with a fast panning shot.

"Let's work it out" was the actor's suggestion.

There were other concessions he wanted. He wanted no cuts to close-ups, no cuts of the feet in motion, no cuts of the shoulders moving, no cuts of isolated parts of the body inserted in the flow of action. It destroyed the concept of the dance. So did overhead shots, weird-angle shots, and straight-down shots from twelve o'clock high.

The camera should shoot about eye level, or perhaps even below that, to give the paying audience just about the same point of view of the person who went to a live musical comedy. To Fred this was essential to the enjoyment of the dance, since it was created to be seen from out front. Dancing was the whole body—or it was nothing.

And when the next Astaire-Rogers picture went in front of the cameras, things were different—and the difference became immediately evident to the expert.

The solution to these difficult problems involved the design of what came eventually to be known as "the Astaire dolly." Since the camera seemed to have its limitations in filming a dance—it tended to shoot better from higher up than at eye level—the floor-level camera dolly was used in the end. But this was later.

Using a dolly on the set created a difficult problem. With the slick Bakelite surfaces of the sets, the presence of dolly wheels on it would mark it and produce wheel tracks.

Bob Cassiday again:

> The problem with the high-gloss surfaces used for the dances was that the Bakelite almost immediately became tracked even if you walked lightly across it. During the filming of a dance sequence, the entire glossy surface had to be washed down with Energine between takes—and there was usually more than one take. You couldn't use oil, even though it would have been faster, because none of the dancers could have worked on an oil-slicked floor. Once a set was constructed, we used to lay light cardboard over every square inch of the floor.
>
> Wheeling a dolly across that surface during a shot would have ruined the gloss. We kept that in mind when we designed the dance sets, although some of them were pretty elaborate and wide angled. The dolly kept the camera at a low level, allowing it to follow the dancers right along as they moved from one end of the set to the other.

A system for photographing an Astaire dance evolved through trial and error. At first three cameras were used on regular dollies— the usual number at the time employed for an ordinary camera setup. For an Astaire dance, all three cameras shot the dancers "straight on." The first, or "A" camera, was usually positioned at the angle Fred considered best; the "B" was placed to the left of that, and the "C" to the right of "A." It was more or less a case of bracketing the dance laterally.

Once the rushes were viewed, Fred and the editor would select the best shot of the three for use in the film. But why bother with three angles? Fred was once asked.

"The 'B' rush, taken a little from one side, sometimes has a more interesting composition than the direct shot," Fred explained.

> One shot may be more "alive" than the next. It is almost impossible to be sure which recording [of the same dance on film] will be the most satisfactory; the eye of the camera is so entirely different from the human eye. It can look at you from different angles, follow you without altering the perspective. If possible, one take will be used for the whole dance. If, however, the "B" take is much better in one sequence, while the "A" is better in another, the best sequences are pieced together, but the sequence of the dance itself is never broken. The audience may be conscious of a

114

change of angle, but it will never be conscious that the flow of the dance has been interrupted.

The Astaire dolly, when it evolved in about 1935, was a distinct departure from this three-camera technique. By that time Fred and his choreographer had a pretty good idea where the best shots could be obtained. The dolly was a one-camera technique. The advantage of the dolly was its low point of origin—the dance was shot below eye level, about two feet from the floor.

H. C. Potter, who directed one of the later Astaire-Rogers movies at RKO described it:

> It was on tiny wheels with a mount for the camera that put the lens about two feet above the ground. On it rode the camera operator and the assistant who changed the focus and that's all. Fred always wanted to keep the camera in as tight as possible, and they used to shoot with a forty-millimeter lens, which doesn't give you too much leeway. So every time Fred and Ginger moved toward us, the camera had to go back, and every time they moved back, the camera went in. The head grip, who was in charge of pushing this thing, was a joy to watch. He would maintain a consistent distance, and when they were in the midst of a hectic dance, that's quite a stunt.

As for recording the dance on the sound track, that took a lot of working out, too. Fred found a satisfactory method only after three or four pictures had been completed. At first the dancers worked to the live sound of an orchestra playing the dance number. Fred found this disconcerting. The sets were so huge that the orchestra was located almost "a block away" in Fred's words, making it difficult to keep in strict time with its beat.

Soon enough another technique was developed. The orchestra would record the entire dance number first and provide a playback for the dancers to rehearse to and shoot the routine to. If there were any tap sections, these would be synchronized later on, with Fred trying to duplicate the sounds with his feet as he watched his movements projected on a screen. These new sounds would then be mixed in with the sounds of the orchestra. The system is similar to "looping," now used universally to correct and/or strengthen bad lines of dialogue or other incongruities.

As Bob Cassiday explained:

> The sharp sound of taps on the gleaming cosmetic surfaces of the dance floor was muffled and dulled by the artificial

surface material. To provide Astaire with a proper dance floor on which his taps would sound bright and bouncy, we built him a special floor in a soundproof closet. The floor was made of tongue-in-groove oak, the same kind used on dance-hall floors, nailed diagonally and tightly into an underlayment of ordinary wood. When Astaire was dubbing in the sound of his taps to the finished shot of the dance, he could get a much better sound from this "natural" surface.

A modus operandi for shooting an Astaire-Rogers picture evolved after a while and became standard after most of the kinks were ironed out. Briefly the schedule went this way:

1. Astaire would work out the dance routines, setting the choreography and rehearsing his steps for about five or six weeks. During this time the dances would be incorporated into the story line of the script.
2. The dramatic scenes would be rehearsed and completed first. This meant the nondancing cast would be finished and out of the way.
3. The less difficult dancing and singing routines would be perfected, shot, and finished.
4. The final big production number—or numbers—would be made.

With the tremendous success of *The Gay Divorcée,* Pandro Berman immediately cast Irene Dunn in *Roberta.* Randolph Scott was set opposite her. There was no way he could have his dance team play the leads; they simply had to play second fiddle in a light, romantic subplot.

The dumbness of the story—an all-American football hero inherits his aunt's chic Parisian fashion house and winds up with a Russian princess who is a fashion designer for a wife—put a lot of pressure on the dance team (to keep all this in the air.) Fred is Scott's buddy, but Ginger plays a nightclub singer posing as a Polish countess! Ye Gods.

Nevertheless, *Roberta* did have a lot going for it. First of all, the music was by Jerome Kern, with "Smoke Gets in Your Eyes" the big number from the Broadway show. There were also the haunting "Yesterdays," sung by Dunne, and the memorable and now classic "Lovely to Look At," also by Dunne and reprised by Astaire and Rogers in a marvelous dance. Plus "I Won't Dance," by Dorothy Fields, Oscar Hammerstein II, and Jerome Kern, a number that, with a different lyric by Hammerstein, had been used in a 1934 London musical called *Three Sisters.*

The lilting classic "Lovely to Look At" was written especially for the movie, with Dorothy Fields supplying the lyrics. It was only half as long as most pop songs of the time—sixteen measures to the usual thirty-two. Pandro Berman was a bit concerned with this odd length, and he discussed the number with Kern.

BERMAN: Isn't it possible for you to make the song just a wee bit longer:
KERN: That's all I had to say.

The show was approached in a new vein for Hollywood; no one in the original Broadway show played in the movie. Bob Hope's role went to Fred Astaire. Lyda Roberti's role went to Ginger Rogers. Tamara's went to Irene Dunne. Ray (then Raymond) Middleton's role went to Randolph Scott. Sydney Greenstreet's role went to Ferdinand Munier. George Murphy's role was written out.

There were changes—some minor, some major. Parts of the lyrics offended the Hays Office. In "Let's Begin," sung by Fred et al., the original lines contained an interesting observation about a young lady having "necked until she was wrecked." That was changed to an innocuous reference to a meeting for which there would be "no reason for vain regret."

The major change was in the addition of the Astaire-Rogers romance. Ginger Rogers's role, originally a sideline vamp sent in to stir up the hero, was built up to that of a fake countess, in reality a nightclub singer. Fred's role of the band leader was built up considerably.

There were some abject gags that have not weathered time well. Randolph Scott tells his aunt, Helen Westley, that he has broken his engagement to his fiancée:

"She's given me the air. We had a row."

His aunt laughs. "Oh, I thought you said she'd given you an heir."

Another "priceless" gem:

"You may call me Tanka," says the fake Polish countess (Ginger).

"Tanka?"

"You're welcome."

Ouch!

A Russian nobleman acting as the hotel doorman gets in a verbal battle with Randolph Scott:

"I'm still the boss of this outfit," Scott shouts, "and you're fired!"

"No, no. I am not fired," insists the prince. "I am perfectly cool."

But there was one nice one in the lines written for Fred: "John," he tells his cloddish buddy Randolph Scott, "every day you act worse. But today you're acting like *tomorrow*."

"I'll Be Hard to Handle," a duet by Astaire and Rogers, is sung and then danced at the "Café Russe"—an Art Deco version of a Parisian boîte complete with elevated bar, wide, curving steps leading up to it, and a snazzy black-ice dance-floor surface criss-crossed with thin white lines. The costumes are all black and white to carry out the decor: Ginger in flared pants and white blouse; Fred in black pants, black-and-white shoes, and white shirt.

"I Won't Dance" is spectacular. Starting out as a nasty piano duet by Fred and his rehearsal pianist, Hal Borne—in a style he calls "feelthy piano"—it becomes a duet with Ginger as she shimmies up in a lamé silver gown that shows off her hair and figure. She pleads with him to do a dance solo; he resists and finally does an amalgam of toe steps, spinning pirouettes, and clattery tap clusters that are tap pyrotechnics at their best.

The big number of the show is "Smoke Gets in Your Eyes," appearing twice, first sung by Dunne in what is supposed to be a rendition of "an old Russian proverb," ("When your heart's on fire, smoke gets in your eyes.") It is reprised later in the film by a Fred-and-Ginger dance. It's a romantic adagio in which she is dressed in backless black to Fred's formal tails. It's short and its sweet—a few steps, a plunge, a recover, and it's over.

"Lovely to Look At" is a fashion-show number Kern wrote for the movie. Dunne sings it, introducing her new fall line. The gowns are worn by a number of bit players—one of whom is Lucille Ball! Ball later went on to star in the television hit *Lucy*, and with her then husband, Desi Arnaz, she purchased the studio that RKO had become and turned it into Desilu Productions.

"I Won't Dance" is a special treat seconds before the fadeout, a kind of tease to see the next Astaire-Rogers film with music by Irving Berlin—*Top Hat*.

Roberta is generally forgotten in the long line of Astaire-Rogers movies. Reason: the libretto, taken from the Broadway "hit," is pretty heavy going. Irene Dunne and Randolph Scott are both burdened by clanking plot needs; they are hardly people at all. Fred and Ginger, on the other hand, are free wheeling types who come off better than the leads do. Another reason for the scarcity of *Roberta* on television is that it was purchased by M-G-M from RKO so that Metro could make an update of it; it lay on the shelves for years without being rereleased anywhere.

By now it had become obvious that the Astaire-Rogers team was being welded into a consolidated, integrated *unit*. Ginger Rogers, in spite of her ridiculous accent in the picture—at least she had the taste to play it so broad it was obviously a put-on—was getting laughs on her own. But it was in her dancing and in her relationship with Fred Astaire that she was becoming more her own person.

The gun-chewing, sarcastic, snippity-young-woman image she had brought to Hollywood—and had continued to project even in the first scenes of *Rio* and *The Gay Divorcée*—were gone, honed to an edge by her work with Fred. The old cliché that he gave her class and she gave him sex was being proved out. Indeed, her work with him had elevated her far above her beginnings.

When *Roberta* opened in 1935, the critics were ecstatic. *Time* magazine wrote:

> The most pleasant moments in *Roberta* arrive when Fred Astaire and Ginger Rogers turn the story upside down and dance on it. On the three occasions when they allow their feet to speak for them, their sleek and nimble scufflings lift *Roberta* out of the class of ordinary entertainment and make it an intermittent masterpiece. The picture establishes Fred Astaire more firmly than ever as the number one hoofer of the cinema and proves what *The Gay Divorcée* suggested: that Ginger Rogers is a wholly acceptable partner.

Andre Sennwald, in the *New York Times:*

> With the excellent help of Professor Astaire, the Kublai Khans at RKO have erected a bright and shimmering pleasure dome. The work is a model of urbanity in the musical films and Mr. Astaire, the debonair master of light comedy and the dance, is its chief ornament. To watch them skipping on effortless cat's feet across a dance floor is to experience one of the major delights of the contemporary cinema. . . . If there is a flaw in the photoplay it is the unfortunate circumstance that Mr. Astaire and his excellent partner, Miss Rogers, cannot be dancing during every minute of it.

Sennwald even had good words for the dialogue: "The libretto, which proved a definite handicap to *Roberta* on the stage, has been visibly brightened by the dialogue polishers in the studio."

Well, sort of.

A look at the financial records at the studio gives another indication of the reason the team worked so well together. *Flying Down to Rio* was the biggest money-maker in the history of the studio. Its profits were $480,000—not much in today's economy, but in that Depression-ridden world, it was a tremendous sum, and it was *net*. *The Gay Divorcée* eclipsed it, of course, bringing in $584,000. *Roberta* went even higher: $770,000!

"They were tremendous moneymakers for us in the sense that it was the worst time in the history of the film business," Producer Pandro Berman recalled.

No pictures were doing the kind of business they came to do later in the 1930s. For example, one million *gross* was considered tremendous by M-G-M, the biggest company in the business with the biggest stars. These pictures starred people like Garbo, Joan Crawford, Gable, Wallace Beery, Marie Dressler, people like that. If they did one million, that was tremendous. Well, we did three million dollars with the first Fred Astaire movie, and we did the same with the next five or six. I guess that's the equivalent of maybe forty million today, in terms of today's costs and today's market. The pictures pulled us out of bankruptcy. They made us go into profit. And that was fabulous.

It was during the filming of *Roberta* that Fred began getting closer and closer to the technical end of the business of making pictures. He would spend hours in the cutting rooms, trying to make sure that the sound was right and in synch with his taps.

Irene Dunne was aware of his dedication to his art. "Fred was known as the number-one worrier in Hollywood. He was such a perfectionist about his routines. He was always a pleasure to work with, but heaven help anyone who didn't do his job well."

It was during *Roberta* that Fred arrived at Jerome Kern's house one night to show him what he had done with one of the numbers in the show. He began dancing the number and danced right on through Kern's palatial house. For his numbers in *Roberta*, Fred spent *nine weeks* in rehearsal.

Getting the dances from the inside of his head onto the final film was what Fred was able to do better than anyone else in the business—then and probably since. How did he do it?

Chapter Ten

Putting on His Top Hat

He was born Hermes Panagiotopulos in Nashville, Tennessee, where he grew up, a loose-jointed, dark-haired young man of Greek background who wanted to dance—not an unusual thing for a lad of Greek extraction. But Hermes wanted to dance not for fun, like most Greeks, but for money and fame. His father was the Greek consul in Nashville.

At fourteen, the good-looking young teenager left the South and traveled to New York, where he began looking for work on the Broadway stage. In order to facilitate his search, he changed his last name to "Pan," making his name an odd combination of two Greek dieties. Hermes, the god of good luck (among other things), and Pan, the satyr.

He got work in the chorus of the first show in which Ginger Rogers danced and sang, *Top Speed*. Before he was twenty, Pan was acting as assistant dance director on several musical-comedy productions in Manhattan. Two years later he was in Hollywood, performing the same chores at various studios.

He was selected by Dave Gould as assistance dance director for *Flying Down to Rio*, in which he became Fred's faithful alter dancing ego. But he was also a hardworking assistant director, running forty chorus girls through their paces before he could spend five minutes with Fred.

Pan worked without credit for two pictures but finally was listed in the credits of the third Astaire-Rogers picture, *The Gay Divorcée*. Fred knew he needed someone to keep him more or less in line, someone who knew dancing as well as he did.

"Fred Astaire creates his own numbers to a great extent," wrote a reporter for *American Dance* magazine. "No dancer, no matter how great he is, or how clever, can correct himself. He must have someone to assist and criticize him if he is to grow and be successful, and this is what Hermes Pan does for Fred Astaire."

And so the real god Hermes—in his role as god of luck—was watching over both Fred and the young dance director when they met on the RKO sound stage in 1933. Very soon, once the Astaire-Rogers alliance was forged, Fred and Hermes worked out a general work routine that enabled them to get Fred's dances created and set.

Astaire once wrote about the agonizing throes of making up a simple dance routine:

> You go to a rehearsal hall months ahead. . . . When you come in you don't know *anything* of what you're going to do. . . . For maybe a couple of days we [Hermes Pan, Ginger Rogers, and Fred Astaire] wouldn't get anywhere— just stand in front of a mirror and fool around. . . . Then suddenly I'd get an idea, or one of them would get an idea. . . . So then we'd get started. . . . There was no telling when you might finish. You might get practically the whole idea of the routine done that day, but then you'd work on it, edit it, scramble it, and so forth. It might take sometimes as long as two, three weeks to get something to do.
>
> After we got going, [Ginger] would say, "How about this?" and I'd say, "Fine, we'll use it."

Mark Sandrich, who directed many of the Astaire-Rogers pictures, once remarked, "You would be surprised how much [Ginger Rogers] adds to the numbers. Fred arranges them, and then, when they get to rehearsing, Ginger puts in her own suggestions. And they're sensible ones. Fred discusses every one with her at length, and a good many of them are used."

Ginger once made the rather modest remark "We all pitched in."

A more exuberant account of what it meant to work with Fred came out in a 1966 interview with Ginger Rogers:

> How do you think those Astaire routines were accomplished? With mirrors? . . . Well, I thought I knew what concentrated work was before I met Fred, but he's the limit. Never satisfied until every detail is right, and he will not compromise. No, sir! What's more, if he thinks of something better after you've finished a routine, you do it over. . . . He may get a hunch in the middle of the night. And he doesn't confine his mental gymnastics to dancing. Sometimes he'll think of a new line of dialogue or a new angle for the story. Ask the boys around the studio. They never know what time of night he'll call up and start ranting enthusiastically about a

fresh idea. . . . No loafing on the job of an Astaire picture, and no cutting corners.

"It's different from a musical comedy," Pan once said.

A musical comedy starts from scratch and opens five weeks later. Featured dancers in such shows can perfect routines long after the show has opened, changing them for the better, working at every public performance eight times a week.

In pictures, it has to be done first. Astaire and Rogers use at least eight weeks blocking out the routines and practicing them. At the end of those eight weeks, the filming begins. Even before the cameras, the dancers make mistakes. Some of the smoothest dances would be shot even as much as forty times before the perfect one came along.

The general formula for creating a dance routine would begin with a preliminary study of the story line of the picture. When the first scenario was typed up, it was delivered to the special stage set aside for Astaire to work in, and there Astaire, Rogers, and Pan would read the script together. This would give them a feel for what the picture was going to be about and an understanding of the kind of characters they would be playing.

Immediately after that they would go into a music room, where they would hear the score for the show—if Fred had not heard it all before. If anything seemed to be lacking in the music, Fred would immediately talk to the composer with ideas of one kind or another. And from that moment on, Fred would be thinking—along with Hermes Pan.

Then came the hard part: getting the steps in order. For at least two weeks Ginger Rogers was not involved; she was usually working on another picture. Hers were usually shot between the big Astaire-Rogers productions.

"We just fool around, just fool around for hours," Pan once said about the creative period. And out of that fooling around, a few steps would begin to emerge. On the basis of these, choreographer and dancer would work together for days, usually without a routine and without taking any definite aim. Luck and trial and error would usually bring them something new.

"I would play Rogers for the first two weeks," Pan said. "I know how she dances and what she expects from Astaire. I'm her reverse side. Sometimes I play Astaire."

After two weeks of this intensive creative effort, Ginger Rogers would appear for work. And nerves would begin to tighten up in about the third week. By then most of the set steps had been worked out, at least in outline, for the basic routines. But tempers would begin to flare and boil. And it would be Pan who would have to put them through their paces and criticize, criticize, criticize.

"It's not easy to tell Fred that he's doing something wrong. He's a perfectionist, and that's the worst thing a perfectionist can hear. Yet if he doesn't hear it, he's not a perfectionist."

By the end of the fourth week, everything was usually pretty well set—that is, the routines were all penciled in.

Now followed more weeks of hard, intensive, unrelenting practice, day and night, until the feet were bleeding, temperaments were ragged, and there might even be tears and groans and shouts. But by the end of this rugged period, the dancers would be letter-perfect, able to dance all the routines in their sleep. They would be so perfect that they would carry on automatically even if some crisis developed. There was no telling which take would be the perfect one.

The actual effort of creating the dance steps was not in the final analysis the *reason* for the success of the Astaire-Rogers films. There was *more* than perfection that made them good. Fred once said:

> If I may say it, the success of the majority of my dances has been due in great measure to the fact that I have introduced my numbers not only at the psychological moment [in a story line] but in a manner that would logically blend with the ideas of the play.

In other words, Fred insisted that the dances be integrated into the action and flow of the story idea itself:

> To catch the public dances must have a personality and a pattern. The times my dances have clicked are the times they had a reason, when they told a part of the story, and when they belonged in the plot. It is extremely important for a dance cue to flow naturally into and out of the story. . . . Each dance ought to spring somehow out of a character or situation."

For some time now, Fred had been toying with the idea of updating an old gag he had found quite effective in the failed Broadway musical *Smiles*. This was a neat piece of business of shooting down a bunch of men in top hats with his black cane as a machine gun. He had told Mark Sandrich about the concept, and Sandrich had liked the idea.

With the great success of Cole Porter's "Night and Day" number in *The Gay Divorcée* and with the obvious success of the Jerome Kern score in *Roberta*, the studio was casting around for another composer to sign up for the next Astaire-Rogers picture. Through the grapevine, Sandrich heard that Irving Berlin might be available. He was one of the most talented songwriters of the era, but he seemed to be in a slump in the middle nineteen thirties. Sandrich called him in and signed him up for two new projects—he was glad to be working with Astaire, Berlin said. One of the ideas was the "machine gun" number, but Berlin was more intrigued by the idea of the chorus of guys in top hats.

"A getting-dressed number," Berlin murmured. He scribbled some words down on a piece of paper. "Putting on my top hat. Tying up my white tie. Brushing off my tails."

By that time, both Sandrich and Berlin had the name for the show: *Top Hat*. And, oddly enough, it certainly fit Fred Astaire to a T. Who else better? When Fred heard the title, he was instantly enthusiastic.

To write the original script, Sandrich hired Dwight Taylor, who had written the original play on which *The Gay Divorcée* was based. Taylor went to work and began to fashion a story much in the same style of *The Gay Divorcée*. In fact, the story that emerged had most of the same elements in it: mistaken identity, juvenile love, the old ABC structure (attraction, breakup, and conciliation). The ABC structure is of course the old Hollywood plot gimmick: boy meets girl, boy loses girl, boy gets girl.

Taylor's story line has Fred meeting and instantly falling in love with Ginger, pursuing her, winning her over in a dance, losing her through the mistaken-identity device, and getting her back when all the confusion is ultimately cleared up.

Sound familiar?

Handed the first draft of the story, Fred was appalled. He attached this note to the script as he handed it back to Pandro Berman:

> In the first place—as this book is supposed to have been written *for me* with the intention of giving me a chance to do the things that are most suited to me—I cannot see that my part embodies any of the necessary elements except to *dance-dance-dance*.
>
> I am cast as a *straight juvenile* & rather a cocky and arrogant one at that—a sort of objectionable young man without charm or sympathy or humor.
>
> I cannot see that there is any real story or plot to this script.

It is a series of events patterned *too closely after Gay Divorce* without the originality & suspense of that play.

I have practically no comedy of any consequence except in the scene in the cab.

I am forever pawing the girl or she is rushing into my arms. . . .

After I go to the Lido—I dissolve into practically *nothing*—it seems, saying or doing nothing at all interesting or humorous. The lead into "Cheek to Cheek" is hopeless as at present designed. It would be impossible to get a sincere note into that number out of the situation which precedes it. The fact that Rogers *slaps me in the face* in two different episodes is certainly wrong. . . .

At least when Fred Astaire wrote notes, people read them. Taylor saw the points Fred had brought up and worked hard on the script to bring it up to the sparkling standard of the final for *The Gay Divorcée*. To cover all bets, the studio hired a rewrite man for Taylor to back up his work and assist in changing it. His name was Allan Scott, a playwright himself; his farce *Goodbye Again* had run for two performances on Broadway the same year *The Gay Divorce* played there.

The basic "mistake" of *Top Hat*'s plot, Rogers's mistaken conception that Astaire is the husband of her best friend, is given a lengthy study from various angles in the final rewrite of the script. Incidentally, both Taylor and Scott were coauthors but did not work together. Sandrich acted as editor and overseer of the operation. Whatever, the resulting script by Taylor and Scott was eventually a bubbling, effervescent confection—perfect for the cast assembled to breathe life into it.

"If at first you do succeed, do it again": RKO was following that old Hollywood adage in casting *Top Hat*. Edward Everett Horton is Fred's bumbling "Uncle Dudley" sidekick again. Eric Blore is the meddling English butler; Erik Rhodes is the Italian bottom pincher. Helen Broderick is new to the team, playing the same kind of part Alice Brady played in *The Gay Divorcée*. With a difference. Broderick's corner-of-the-mouth delivery of her nicely barbed lines adds a new dimension to the team surrounding Fred and Ginger.

Irving Berlin wrote six songs for the picture, or rewrote some he had lying around. Of these six tunes, one was dropped because it made the picture too long. It was later resurrected for the next Astaire-Rogers picture, *Follow the Fleet*.

Berlin surpassed himself. Every single one of the five numbers in the picture became a hit song! This was a success previously undreamed of for a Hollywood movie. The five songs are now standards of one degree or another. On September 28, 1935, the radio show *Your Hit Parade* featured all five Berlin songs in the top fifteen for the week.

This phenomenal achievement reactivated Berlin and got him back on the high road once again. Most of his time would be spent writing musical scores of movies from that date (1935) on.

Fred had danced to Berlin tunes since 1915, but he did not meet the songwriter until they were making *Top Hat*. A lifelong friendship developed. Berlin once called Astaire his "closest and best friend." Eventually, Berlin would supply songs for six Astaire movies—more than any other composer. "He's a real inspiration for a writer," Berlin said of Fred. "I'd never have written *Top Hat* without him. He makes you feel secure."

Choreographer Hermes Pan was assigned to the picture as fullfledged dance director. It was his reward for working without recognition on two pictures and as assistant on one more.

Because the songs were written while the story was being assembled, each story and its lyric carries forward the story line easily and effortlessly.

"No Strings," the first routine, is a most pleasant romantic meeting of two lovers. Astaire, happily telling bumbling Horton how good it is to be a bachelor—"No Strings, I'm Fancy Free!"—breaks into a dance in his London hotel room. Below him, Ginger Rogers hears the noise with a great deal of annoyance, springing into action when a hunk of plaster clobbers her. When she confronts Astaire, the two stare at one another and go into a duet. Of course, from that moment on it is Fred's dream to exchange bachelorhood for marriage to Ginger.

"Isn't It a Lovely Day" follows as Fred begins to pursue Ginger. On a horseback ride in Hyde Park, London, a storm breaks out, and Ginger, in riding clothes, and Fred, in a lounge suit, seek shelter in a deserted bandstand. This is a stylized Art Deco RKO bandstand, American and glitzy, with marvelous curlicues and elaborate designs. Hyde Park it is *not*, but no matter. In this setting, the courtship begins in earnest in a witty game of terpsichorean flirtation. At the end, instead of kissing Ginger, Fred, with typical understatement, shakes hands with her.

"Top Hat, White Tie, and Tails" comes next. It is the epitome of the getting-dressed dances made famous by Fred Astaire. It is, in the view of most dance experts, Astaire's "signature piece." It relies on his ability to switch tempo and stance from one moment to the next, varying exuberant activity with motionless waiting. It is danced before a vague stage backdrop depicting the Eiffel Tower in sketched outline. A chorus of top-hatted men lounge about as Astaire sings the number and begins his dance. They imitate his every move. He gives them harder things to do. They follow him. Finally, he dances away from them, surpassing them symbolically. The stage darkens menacingly; the mood is threatening. The chorus suddenly and dangerously reappears, and Astaire dispatches them one by one with his magic cane.

This was a big number for Astaire, and he knew it. His new acquaintance, another crack dancer, James Cagney, was visiting the set at the time of the filming of the dance. Fred did the first solo but didn't think it was right. He did it again. After the third take, Cagney whispered to Astaire:

"Don't shoot it again, kid—you got it on the second take. You'll never top that one."

But the taskmaster insisted on another take. The dance was shot yet again. In the end, viewing the rushes next morning, Fred discovered that Cagney was right. It *was* number two. The epitome of dance for Astaire, judged so by another master of the art.

At this point the scene of the movie switches to Venice. Plot nuances have convinced Ginger that Fred is the husband of Helen Broderick, who is actually married to Horton. Rogers goes to Venice to inform Broderick of her "husband's" philandering—with Ginger!

When Pandro Berman and Mark Sandrich had at first discussed sending a camera crew to Venice, Italy, to film establishing shots the way they had done for *Flying Down to Rio* earlier, they realized that it would be next to impossible. Mussolini was in firm control of Italy. Americans were not welcome. The solution was simple: They called in Polglase from the art department.

"Build us Venice," they told him.

And he did.

Although a monumental undertaking, it was the perfect setting for the inspired craziness of "The Piccolino," about which more in detail later. RKO devoted two entire sound stages to "Venice," connecting them together. The set is a mad mélange of stylized Venetian barber poles, weird bridges over black-dyed water, circles and curlicues of white against black flooring, wild medieval designs in Art Deco rectangles and triangles, and foliage potted in cubes with cabalistic designs etched on them.

"There was no Venice ever like that, but nobody who saw the picture seemed to mind!" one of the camera crew remarked later.

"Cheek to Cheek" is one of the most romantic numbers that Fred and Ginger ever did. It takes place in Venice, RKO style. Fred dressed in immaculate formal attire. Ginger is in a gown of light turquoise satin, accented with feathers.

And thereby hangs a tale.

Fred had enough experience with dancers and their costumes to know that it was not just Ginger who wanted to come out in something astounding and eye-catching.

"*All* girls try to add to their costumes at the last minute," he once said. The purpose was obvious. They used blinding bangles and sparkling sequins to attract the attention of the audience away from—well—away from Fred.

Through the years Fred came to feel that one of the most skilled at diverting the eye away from him was Ginger Rogers, aided and abetted by her mother, Lela. Fred knew Lela from those New York days; she had now come to be considered one of the most formidable backstage mothers in the annals of show business by the people around RKO. She worked at the studio, running a drama school for neophyte females and coaching starlets like Lucille Ball and Betty Grable in the facts of cinema craft. But she did watch over her daughter's career with the eye of a hawk. Part of her vigilance concerned Ginger's dress.

Pandro Berman said, "We'd plan the costumes in advance, but then Lela would work on the designer, and we'd never know what monstrosity Ginger would show up in."

During rehearsals Ginger would usually be in slacks and shirt-waist, and the dance steps would never be impeded by swirling skirts or whatever. So Fred and Hermes Pan never had any idea what her final outfit would be. And this time, when she showed up in—

Pan recalled the details. "We were ready to go with the 'Cheek to Cheek' number when Ginger arrived in this dress. It was covered with ostrich feathers from neck to hem. It was late in the afternoon, and we were to shoot the number early the next morning."

Fred and Ginger began to rehearse the steps, but the feathers started to moult all over the set. It was a blizzard.

"The feathers flew all over the place. They blinded Fred and got in his nose and made him sneeze. After about an hour, he gave up."

FRED: I thought those feathers were supposed to be sewn to this dress.
DESIGNER: Oh, it's only because it was the first time the dress was moved around a bit. It won't happen again.

Fred was suspicious. He called a meeting the following morning, when shooting was scheduled. "The dress designer assured us it would be okay," Pan recalled.

They went ahead with the routine, but the feathers were still swirling. After each try at a take, the floor had to be swept, then mopped, then dried. Then the dance would begin, and the feathers would fly again. By now Lela was hovering about, obviously anticipating trouble.

Pan said:

Late in the afternoon, Fred threw up his hands. He was white with anger. He yelled something at Ginger. She burst into tears, and Lela came charging at Fred like a mother rhinocerous protecting her young. After a lot of hollering, Fred retired to one side of the sound stage, and Ginger and Lela settled down on the other.

As Pan recalled, "For the whole day there was stony silence."

What happened was that the impasse between the principals was resolved by the intervention of almost everyone else on the picture. The designer finally agreed to stay up all night sewing each feather into place.

On the third day, there were still feathers flying, but the camera crew finally got a sight on Fred and Ginger.

Fred referred to the incident in his autobiography, but he treated it very lightly, as if it were great fun. He mentioned that Phyllis, along with David Niven, who was an RKO contract actor at the time and who had become a fast friend of the Astaires, was on the set watching the filming when Ginger appeared in the gown.

"She looks like a wooster!" Phyllis said; she always had trouble with her r's. She and Niven finally left to avoid the "embarrassing" situation that arose. In Fred's version, it was only embarrassment. He and Pan took the whole thing lightly, even composing a gag duet to the tune of "Cheek to Cheek:"

Feathers—I hate feathers—
And I have them so that I can hardly speak,
And I never find the happiness I seek
With those chicken feathers dancing
Cheek to Cheek.

And then, he said, he and Pan took to calling Ginger "Feathers."

It was a bit more serious than he made out. How serious may be determined by Ginger herself, who was still very defensive about that dress years later. Yes, she *loved* it. She *approved* of it. "When it was finally seen on the screen, everyone who had been dead against it loved it, approved of it, and of course now it's recognized as one of the loveliest dresses I've ever worn."

Irving Berlin had a great time writing "The Piccolino," the monumental production number designed to wrap up the movie.

It's a neat tongue-in-cheek parody of the earlier "big" Astaire-Rogers dances: "The Caricoca" and "The Continental."

Hermes Pan was trying to work out the steps for the thing when he suddenly noticed that the song was really about a tune and not a dance. He pointed out to the composer, "Come to the Casino / And hear them play the Piccolino." Shouldn't it be a *dance* number?

Berlin was immediately inspired. "I'll change the name of the tune to 'The Lido,' " he told Pan, "and then the lyric can run: 'Come and do the Lido / It's very good for your libido.' "

"The Piccolino" was a mad hodgepodge of a dance, including a huge gondola parade, a large dancing chorus, a go at the lyrics by Ginger, a duet by Fred and Ginger, and a finish with the two of them doing a dance in a two-minute routine taken without cuts. And everybody else in Venice appeared at one point or another. Probably everybody in Europe, too.

"I love it," Irving Berlin said about this song of his, however tongue in cheek it was. "I love it, the way you love a child that you've had trouble with. I worked harder on 'Piccolino' than I did on the whole score."

The team of Astaire and Rogers would never be better than in this picture. They had reached their apex. It was such a great film that it could probably never be reprised properly.

In fact, it never was.

Chapter Eleven

At the Peak

With *Top Hat*, the team of Astaire-Rogers was at its peak. It was one of the hottest items in show-business history. The *New York Daily News* even praised the achievement of *Top Hat* in its editorial columns:

> The best thing yet done in movie musical comedy. The music is Berlin at his best; the settings are gorgeous; the lines are among the funniest we've heard, and the dancing and comedy of Fred Astaire and Ginger Rogers are something to go back and see again. Especially the dancing.

Accolades, accolades, accolades. But in a much more important area, Fred was profiting admirably from the escalating successes of his pictures. And in dollars.

He had made about $10,000 for his stint in *Flying Down to Rio*. This amount doubled for each of his next two films—*The Gay Divorcée* and *Roberta*—that is, $20,000 for each of them. With *Top Hat* that figure was doubled once again to $40,000.

But with *Top Hat* there was an additional perk. With his consummate and instinctive sense of timing, Fred knew exactly when to bargain, and he did so just prior to *Top Hat*. He was one of the first actors in Hollywood who was able to get himself a percentage of the gross. But Pandro Berman knew what he had; Fred knew that Berman knew. And he was in for a "piece of the action" in the terms of the gangster pictures of the era.

He hit exactly the right time to dicker, because in terms of net profits, *Top Hat* was also the peak. From that picture on, the profits were to be less and less.

For artistry, for popularity, for profitability, *Top Hat* must be considered the watershed of the Astaire-Rogers magic. It was a composite of all the choreographic genius of Astaire, his ability to act in light comedy, his talent for singing and dancing.

There was no reason to question Berman's choice of continuing to make pictures that contained ultimately the same ingredients for the team. That meant serviceable, polished, and punchy screen scenarios; the best pop songs by the best writers; the glittering Art Deco sets that distinguished RKO's art department; top choreographic direction and assistance for Fred.

It is surprising to note that the Astaire-Rogers team would make only five RKO pictures together after *Top Hat*: *Follow the Fleet, Swing Time, Shall We Dance, Carefree,* and *The Story of Vernon and Irene Castle.* Their last costarring vehicle would be *The Barkleys of Broadway,* made in the postwar period for another studio.

Those five pictures featured Astaire and Rogers at the peak of their talent, doing all the things they could do best and inventing new things to stretch their abilities a little more. And Berman showcased the best people he could find to enhance their image.

Follow the Fleet, made in 1936, was the studio's answer to those Americans who felt that since Fred Astaire spent most of his time in white tie and tails he must not be much of a man. With the Depression still hanging on everywhere in spite of the New Deal's attempts to neutralize it, people might not like to see their entertainers decked out in the clothes of the hated and envied rich.

Fleet was a remake of an early play called *Shore Leave,* written by Hubert Osborne and produced by David Belasco. The original involves a spinster dressmaker who falls in love with a sailor named Bilge Smith and renovates an old salvaged ship just for him; he's too proud to accept and sails off, only to return to marry her.

In 1927, Herbert Fields, Clifford Grey, and Leo Robin, with composer Vincent Youmans, turned this play into the smash musical *Hit the Deck.* Three years later RKO made the musical with Polly Walker and Jack Oakie. Still owning the property, RKO now polished it off and handed it to Dwight Taylor and Allan Scott for an update. Berman had signed on Irving Berlin for two pictures, and this was going to have Berlin songs—one of which, "Get Thee Behind Me, Satan," had been dropped from *Top Hat.*

The new story added Fred Astaire as a buddy of Bilge's, with Bilge played by Randolph Scott; it also added Ginger Rogers as a sister of the spinster of the early version of the story. Fred and Ginger supposedly are vaudeville song-and-dancers who broke up when Fred went to sea. The songs and dances fit in nicely.

Harriet Hilliard plays the spinster. She later married Ozzie Nelson, for whom she had worked as a singer in front of his dance band; the two of them went on to longtime fame in radio and television as *Ozzie and Harriet*. Her songs are "Get Thee Behind Me, Satan" and "But Where Are You?" two romantic Berlin numbers.

The centerpiece of the picture is the dance-rehearsal routine staged on board the spinster's ship. The plot has advanced to the point where the hoary old "Let's put on a show!" device is inserted to motivate a musical show on the deck of the newly refurbished ship. After a marvelous barrelhouse rendition by Fred at the piano of "I'm Putting All My Eggs in One Basket," he and Ginger get together for a "rehearsal"—she in slacks, he in sea garb. The ancient vaudeville wheeze in this one comes off fine in their hands: At every new move Fred makes, Ginger becomes so absorbed in the previous step that she continues on with it, bemused, while he goes on with a new one. Then he waits, and she comes to and follows him. Repeat. The routine ends with a parody of the vivacious finales used by dance teams to milk applause from slumbering audiences.

The show within the show features "Let's Face the Music and Dance." Fred has lost all his money at the Monte Carlo Casino and wanders out onto the casino terrace, which is—like Venice in *Top Hat*—strictly a vision of the RKO art department. The wide balcony sports an elegant glass-, chrome-, an ebony-paneled tower, apparently enclosing some kind of interior habitation, brightly illuminated from inside. Beyond that sparkles the Mediterranean, with festoons of gay white lights strung from one end of the sky to the other.

Fred pantomimes despondency, takes a pistol out of his pocket, contemplates it, then suddenly sees Rogers about to leap from the terrace to her death. Together they—well, face the music, and dance. In his white tie and tails, Fred looks more at home in this portion of the picture than in his skivvies; Ginger is pliant and absolutely ravishing in her beaded gown with the huge flaring sleeves.

And thereby hangs an anecdote. Fred was not used to dancing with Ginger while she wore the beaded gown; to keep the flared sleeves down, the costume department had added weights at the wrists. At one point right at the beginning of the dance, the right sleeve smashed against Fred's head, leaving him, as he later put it, practically senseless. And yet, in spite of that, he went on dancing and completed the routine right through to its end.

When it was over, he demanded another take. In fact, there were numbers of takes, some thirty in all. Finally, he had the set closed down, and everybody went home.

In the morning—you guessed it—the rushes showed that the

first take was the best. It was used. Look carefully. You can't see her hit him, but you can see him rather glassy eyed in one portion.

The incredible thing is that he was so practiced in the steps and in the routine that he could continue with it, step for perfect step, even though he was reeling from the blow.

The critics were mixed on this show, with Richard Watts, Jr., of the *New York Herald-Tribune,* claiming that "the score and the dancing are at least up to the enchantment of *Top Hat.*" Frank S. Nugent, in the *New York Times,* wrote:

> Even though it is not the best of the series, it is still good enough to take the head of this year's class in song and dance entertainment. The screen's premier team taps as gayly, waltzes as beautifully, and disagrees as merrily as ever.

Swing Time, the next in the series, is another original screenplay, worked up from a short story by Erwin Gelsey entitled "Portrait of John Garnett." Allan Scott worked on this one with Howard Lindsay. The story concerns a vaudeville star and compulsive gambler down on his luck who misses his wedding to—of all people!—Betty Furness. He flees his creditors and joins up with Ginger Rogers, a dance hostess being pursued by an Erik Rhodes–type lover.

Victor Moore plays Fred's confidant and gambling partner; Eric Blore has a small part as a dance-hall owner. Helen Broderick is Ginger Rogers's confidant.

The music is by Jerome Kern and Dorothy Fields. After a brief dance by Fred—"It's Not in the Cards"—underlining his gambling loss, the pair perform "Pick Yourself Up" in a mock sequence in the dance hall where Fred is pretending not to know anything about dancing. "The Way You Look Tonight" is sung by Fred as he accompanies himself on the piano in Ginger's hotel suite.

The BWS and the centerpiece of the picture is Kern and Fields's marvelous "Waltz in Swing Time," danced as the two audition for a job at the Club Raymond. The scene employs an Art Deco set with a gleaming floor surface over which the dancers simply seem to float. The dance itself is written in waltz time but actually is played in such a way that it seems to "swing." In the words of one expert, it is the team's most virtuosic duet: "It has an almost baroque intricacy."

The dance breaks up into three sections. In the first, the partners are together. In the second, they each do a solo, paralleling each other, touching only incidentally; there is a lot of leaping and hopping. In the third they are together, with Fred side hurdling himself over Rogers's bent body and doing some sweeping fast moves all over the floor.

Ginger Rogers once talked about the number of hours she had spent with Fred Astaire rehearsing their routines for *Swing Time*—350 or so. "The first hundred hours are the most difficult because they are the kindergarten course for the new routines. Once the new steps are learned, it becomes more fascinating to fit them together and perfect the execution of the routines." And they were certainly worth it.

"A Fine Romance" is a nice bantering song sung by the two dancers as they ride in the country in an open car—in a snowstorm!

"Bojangles of Harlem" features Fred in his onetime appearance in blackface. The song is a tribute to Bill Robinson, and the song itself is definitely a dedication to him. He was a popular star of the day, appearing with such stars as Shirley Temple.

"Never Gonna Dance" is performed at the Silver Sandal nightclub, a far more gorgeous and exciting place than the Club Raymond. The floor is a swirl of circles and arcs. From the black surface—Vitrolite—two curving lines of stairs rise to meet in the middle of a higher level to the rear. The black stairs are supported by curving white walls. Tables with glowing white tableclothes are situated on both sides of the stairways. This is a club that should have been built!

Ginger has now agreed to marry the man who is pursuing her, played by George Metaxa, and she tells Fred the truth as she begins to mount the stairs. He bids her good-bye, saying that he's never going to dance again. He sings, she listens, and the dance follows, this one of shattered, impossible love. It is essentially an attempt by Fred to woo Ginger back. The climax occurs as Ginger flees up one staircase, with Fred dancing up the opposite one to intercept her. There, at the top, she escapes him.

To the critics, the picture was mediocre. Howard Barnes felt let down.

It is high time that Fred Astaire and Ginger Rogers were relieved of the necessity of going through a lot of romantic nonsense. The vast success of *Swing Time* is more a tribute to them than to the material of their latest song and dance carnival. They have never performed with more exquisite finish.

After the opening at the Radio City Music Hall, the *Hollywood Reporter* named Fred and Ginger the nation's number-one box-office attraction. However, the figures from the receipts did not bear this out. There seemed to be clouds gathering in the sky above to darken the white sets at RKO.

A lot of talent went into the next picture, *Shall We Dance*. The basic idea came from a short story by Lee Loeb and Harold Buchman, "Watch Your Step." P. J. Wolfson then turned this story into a screen treatment, which in turn was worked up into a screenplay by Allan Scott and Ernest Pagano. For Scott, this was his third Astaire-Rogers movie.

Knowing that the best songwriters in the business were more or less lined up waiting to do pictures for Fred Astaire, Pandro Berman got daring and asked the Gershwin brothers if they would like to do the score for the projected movie. "Daring," because the Gershwins had soured on Hollywood.

They had done a musical for Twentieth Century-Fox called *Delicious* in 1931. It featured Janet Gaynor and Charles Farrell, almost a shoo-in for a box-office hit. Ironically enough, Raoul Roulien, of *Rio* fame, was also in the picture as a Russian (!) composer. Although it did not entirely bomb, it produced no song hits for the Gershwins; they felt they had been burned by the production.

Now, with the Astaire-Rogers thing so hot, Berman was able to sweet-talk them back to Hollywood to do the music for the upcoming picture, then known as *Watch Your Step,* or alternatively, *Stepping Toes* or *Stepping High*.

Berman was on target with the Gershwin brothers. The score is a gold mine of memorable tunes: "Slap That Bass," "They All Laughed," "Let's Call the Whole Thing Off," and "They Can't Take That Away from Me."

Casting followed Berman's original format for the Astaire-Rogers team. Edward Everett Horton is Fred's sidekick again, and Eric Blore reappears.

For a switch, Fred is a ballet dancer named Petroff in this one. Petroff? Actually he is an American *pretending* to be a Russian dancer. He's balletic, but what he wants to do is combine ballroom and tap dancing with ballet's entrechats and arabesques. This story is an *in medias res* job, with Fred having already proposed to Ginger, a musical-comedy star, before the picture starts. On board an ocean liner from France to New York, they are mistaken for man and wife; the joke is that most of their time is spent trying to prove they are *not* married.

Horton is a ballet impressario in charge of Fred's talents. Jerome Cowan plays Rogers's producer. There are some good comic bits: Horton, drunk at a bar on board ship, is asked, "What does your watch say?" and answers, "Tick-tick tick-tick tick-tick." In another, Eric Blore tells his boss, Horton, that he has been arrested. "That's all right," Horton snaps. "We don't need you."

"Beginner's Luck" is a short teaser danced by Fred near the beginning of the film, with "Slap That Bass" the first regular production number. This one is a gimmick dance, Fred performing it in the engine room of the ocean liner, in which he pretends to imitate the engine's workings. According to Hermes Pan, Fred and he were walking past a cement mixer on the RKO lot during a lunch break. "Fred began to dance against the rhythm and just about worked out the routine on the spot." The dance was then written into the script—which, luckily, had an ocean liner in it.

Fred sings "Beginner's Luck" to Ginger, leading up to the song and dance "They All Laughed," performed in a rooftop nightclub. This is a conventional wooing dance and by far the best in the picture. In it Ginger is dressed in a gown that from the waist down sports huge black petaled flowers—or something. Fred is in his usual tails.

Plot complications lead to "Let's Call the Whole Thing Off," a number performed on roller skates after Fred and Ginger sneak off to Central Park and rent them at a concession. Although it wasn't received cordially by the critics or the public, this tour de force, dreamed up by Astaire in his continued search for "different" gimmicks, predates by some years the current rage over *Starlight Express,* an entire musical played on skates!

"They Can't Take That Away from Me" is limited to a vocal rendition by Fred. On a roof-garden dance floor he mounts a combination ballet and jazz dance. It's a beautiful, sleek set, with gleaming white floor and twisty decorations on the walls. At the end of the ballet segment, danced by Harriett Hoctor, she vanishes and is replaced by a chorus of women each wearing a Ginger Rogers mask! The dance continues with Fred trying to find Ginger by unmasking all the dancers. When he finds her, the dance—and the picture—ends.

When they saw the film, George and Ira Gershwin were sorry they had let Berman talk them into doing the songs. "The picture does not take advantage of the songs as well as it should," George wrote a friend. "They literally throw one or two songs away without any kind of plug." He was right; particularly, "Beginner's Luck" is tossed in without fanfare and seems to go up in smoke while the audience waits and waits for the team to *dance* something. Gershwin had a few critical words to say about the stars, too. "This is mainly due to the structure of the story, which does not include any other singers than Fred and Ginger, and the amount of singing one can stand of these two is quite limited."

138

He need not have fretted. A number of the songs he wrote for this film did become solid hits, and several became standards.

The critics were kind. Frank Nugent wrote in the *New York Times:*

> One of the best things the screen's premier dance team has done, a zestful, prancing, sophisticated musical show. It has a grand score by George Gershwin (lyrics by brother Ira), a generous leavening of comedy, a plot or so and, forever, and ever, the nimble hoofing of a chap with quicksilver in his feet and of a young woman who has leapt to follow him with assurance.

The next Astaire-Rogers film was not released until 1938. The team that had produced two pictures in 1935 and 1936 only produced one for the year 1937 and would only produce one for 1938—at least together.

There are three generally acceptable reasons for the slowdown. First of all, the economy was not cooperating with the studio. Although the government was doing all it could to cool the Depression, it wasn't getting very far. People were still out of work in huge numbers. Second, Fred's insistence on not repeating any of his material was posing a definite problem. There were only a certain number of different steps he could come up with. The duet had danced just about every routine, in just about every setting, in just about every story that could be used to carry a musical-comedy score. The third thing was Fred's natural inclination to want to make it on his own; that, coupled with Ginger Rogers's determination to be a dramatic actress and not just half a dance team, provided a good reason for the inevitable slowing down.

To elaborate on point one just a bit: *Top Hat* grossed over $3 million for RKO and made a net profit of $1,325,000—a true bonanza. *Follow the Fleet* dropped off, making a net profit of $945,000—not bad at all, but a definite decline from *Top Hat*. *Swing Time* made a profit of $830,000, more erosion. *Shall We Dance* was a definite falloff, making $413,000. Actually, the next picture in the series, *Carefree*, fared even worse, actually *losing* $68,000!

As for point three, in 1934, Ginger Rogers had made two pictures for RKO, along with *The Gay Divorcée: Rafter Romance* and *Finishing School*. In 1935 she had made three on her own: *Romance in Manhattan, Star of Midnight*, and *In Person*. And, of course, she had teamed with Fred in *Roberta, The Gay Divorcée*, and *Top Hat*. She had been unable to make any alone in 1936. In 1937 both Ginger Rogers and Fred Astaire made films without each other: Rogers, the extremely well-received *Stage Door* with Katharine Hepburn; and Astaire, *A Damsel in Distress*. The latter picture was not well received; it was the first loser Fred was attached to, going in the hole by $65,000.

The sad thing about *Damsel* was that Fred had such high hopes for it. Here he was, pretty much on his own, working to a delightful score by the Gershwin brothers, playing comedy with the team of George Burns and Gracie Allen, kidding around with Ray Noble, a personable English band leader, and teamed with Joan Fontaine, the sister of Olivia de Havilland, who would score on her own later in the Hitchcock classic *Rebecca*.

His "A Foggy Day" is a classic—both his vocal rendition of it and his dance in the mists of London. There's a fun-house episode in the picture that is nicely done. He even did a kind of parody of the old Adele and Fred Broadway "runaround" with Gracie Allen. It is interesting to note, however, that even though Fred's venture on his own lost $65,000, his next effort with Rogers went slightly deeper in the hole, losing $68,000! But then as now, it was the financial stakes that ran things. And on paper Fred looked like a man who was a loser on his own.

Carefree was the only film the team made in 1937. Actually, the picture is really a screwball comedy, with songs and dances added, rather than a well-integrated musical comedy with a book to hold it together. This was to be Mark Sandrich's last film with Astaire and Rogers at RKO. The music was written by Irving Berlin.

Eventually finalized by Ernest Pagano and Allan Scott, the screenplay concerns a psychiatrist asked as a favor to psychoanalyze the girlfriend of a good buddy; in effect, it is a Hollywood wrinkle on the old Miles Standish, John Alden, Priscilla Mullins triangle.

Plans were at first made to hype up the picture—a return of the greatest dancing team in history—with a dream sequence to be filmed in Technicolor. But the studio was losing money again, and Berman decreed that it would not do. Therefore, the dance routine, done to the number Berlin wrote called "I Used to Be Color-Blind," was actually shot in black and white—more or less robbing the lyrics of any point.

Fred's buddy in this one is Ralph Bellamy, surrogate for Randolph Scott/Edward Everett Horton, playing to the hilt the combination bumbling Uncle Dudley and rich wastrel. In the cast is Jack Carson, playing his usual ratchety, snide, gravel-voiced cynic and pal.

Arlene Croce felt that Astaire was "strangely convincing as a psychoanalyst." Clive Hirschhorn, in the *Hollywood Musical*, noted: "Astaire played a psychiatrist (not very convincingly)." Who cares? Actually, in spite of all the "team" work, it turns out to be Ginger Rogers's movie all the way.

Except for a tiny solo at the start, played to Berlin's "Since They Turned Loch Lomond into Swing," which Fred does just before going into a golf-club swinging routine (dance) at the country club, Ginger is in every scene and is required to hold the plot together, too.

But Fred's solo is a marvel. At one point he takes out a harmonica and plays the tune while he is dancing. Another first. Running out of ideas? Hardly!

"I Used to Be Color-Blind" is a dance sequence dreamed by Ginger after Fred has fed her an unbelievable combination of food. Gone is the Art Deco background. One is suddenly in a world of mushrooms, giant ferns, grotesque shrubs, spooky spiderwebs. It's the little people you expect to appear, sure now! But they don't. The set was obviously designed and built before the edict came down from the front office that color was out. It was simply a case of another great idea that got away.

To take the onus off the colorful set filmed in colorless black and white, the dance is shot in part in slow motion—and a lot of it takes place in the air, with jumps, lifts, and leaps across a brook.

The plot calls for Fred to try to hypnotize Ginger in order to break down her inhibitions so she will be susceptible to Bellamy's charms. This is the "Change Partners" routine. Although in a very early routine Fred seems to mesmerize Ginger—in *The Gay Divorcée*'s "Night and Day" number—here he deliberately hypnotizes her.

Although the two of them may have come to this project perhaps with reservations, it doesn't show in their performances. *Carefree* was to be their last picture together at RKO except for *The Story of Vernon and Irene Castle,* a definite departure for Fred. He had always done fiction. Here he was supposed to be doing fact. Yet who better to do the story than Fred and Ginger? For Vernon and Irene Castle were the Fred Astaire and Ginger Rogers of their day.

Since the team is miming another team, the routines simply don't seem like Astaire-Rogers productions. Ginger dresses up in a kind of stylized western outfit, and Fred wears a gray pinstripe suit for "Waiting for the Robert E. Lee," an old standard by L. Wolfe Gilbert and Abel Baer.

Ginger wears a clown costume for the "Yama Yama Man" —black with three white buttons down the middle and a dunce cap on the head with a white tassel on top. Fred plays stooge for a re-creation of an old Lew Fields and Vernon Castle vaudeville skit (*with* Lew Fields) called "The Barber and the Customer."

Probably the most famous routine in the show is "The Castle Walk," performed by Fred and Ginger, along with "The Castle Polka," "The Castle Tango," and "The Castle Waltz."

Even though the ballroom dancing is effortless and captivating, the movie tends to be uneven. One of the best sequences shows the pair dancing across a set that is a giant map of America. Only one song was written specifically for the picture—"Only When You're in My Arms," by Con Conrad, Bert Kalmar, and Harry Ruby.

With *The Story of Vernon and Irene Castle,* Fred Astaire's Ginger Rogers years at RKO were over; they would however, be reunited a decade later at another studio. Fred would now be matched with many of the screen's most exciting dancing partners.

Yet never again would he be so closely identified with a partner as he was during those top-hatted years when he and Ginger Rogers were tapping and twirling their way through the most stylish, lighthearted, Art Deco, black-and-white musicals ever to emerge from Hollywood.

And while they did it, Fred Astaire actually established the motion-picture dance as a specialized kind of art form.

Interlude

At Home with Phyllis

In Hollywood, Fred Astaire was one of the exceptional entertainers who was able to keep his personal life and his professional life completely separated from each other as if by a thick stone wall. It might be said that his professional life *was* his personal life, but that is not quite true, either.

When he was Adele's partner, his personal life was that of a sibling rival to a talented sister. So was his professional life. When Adele left and married and Fred married Phyllis Potter, quite suddenly Fred Astaire had a double life: He was a professional on the set, and he was a human being at home.

He found it not quite so difficult as others to separate those two portions of his life. He had no need for nightlife in California; as he had said, he had already lived a full nightlife in New York and London. Besides that, although Fred never said it, there wasn't the same kind of charge to Los Angeles nightlife as there was to that of New York or London.

In California, Phyllis blossomed. Nowhere near as fragile and gentle as Fred had thought she was when he met her, she put down her roots and began to run the family the way she knew it should be run. In her own quiet way, she was as practical and strong-willed as Fred's mother, Ann Austerlitz.

Hermes Pan once said of her, "Phyllis was just what Fred needed. She became his buffer against the unpleasant things of the world. Fred worshiped and respected her. He phoned her from the studio every day at lunchtime."

Between pictures Fred and Phyllis explored Southern California. Both of them loved to play golf and tennis. Fred could usually beat his wife at golf; but she could take him at tennis. She was also an excellent shot; Fred and she found a wonderful spot to go quail and duck shooting just outside Mexicali—a long drive from L.A. down to Baja California.

143

The Astaires settled down in a big comfortable house on North Alpine Drive at first, one that used to belong to an opera star by the name of Tito Shipa. It was built in the Italian Riviera style— modified with the usual California elements, one of them a swimming pool in the backyard.

Meanwhile, Phyllis began her more serious search for a place where they could build their own home. This search began in earnest at about the time *The Gay Divorcée* was finished and *Roberta* was in the works. By now Fred was in the movie business for better or worse. It certainly looked for the better.

Randolph Scott was a good friend of Fred's and also knew Phyllis well. "Phyllis was utterly feminine and yet a good business executive," he said. "In her own way, she directed their lives, but Fred didn't seem to mind. She'd decide if they'd go marlin fishing or dove hunting in Mexico or just stay at a little motel in Arizona where she'd cook spaghetti for him."

On one of those hunting trips Scott mentioned, Fred heard that Charles Dillingham, the man who had really gotten the Astaires going in the legitimate theater, had died; that was in 1934. Some time after that, Fred got word from his sister Adele that she was expecting a baby toward the end of the year—November 1935, to be precise.

Fred and Phyllis immediately made plans to go to Ireland to see the Cavendishes right after *Top Hat* was finished. They arrived to enjoy a few days at Lismore Castle. The Cavendishes lived in County Waterford, in the north of Ireland. Fred and his brother-in-law, Lord Cavendish, went to the Punchestown races. Both were avid horsemen, and Fred realized that his old interest in racing had never flagged.

During their stop in London after leaving Ireland, Phyllis announced to Fred that she would be expecting a baby in January 1936, and the Astaires immediately booked passage for New York. Fred had taken on a little extracurricular work just for the heck of it: as emcee of the *Lucky Strike Hit Parade* on radio!

Actually, radio was not the medium of expression for Fred's dancing talents, but of course he was a consummate actor by that time as well as an excellent singer. So that his dancing could not be entirely overlooked in his radio appearances, Fred devised a method of conveying taps by sound only.

He had built for him a small wooden platform four feet square that stood about two inches from the floor. A small microphone was placed about two feet off the floor near the dance platform. When the time came for the "dance" number, Fred would sing into his regular standup microphone and tap out the steps on the platform as the "dance" began.

"I found that the only effective steps for radio were those with a lot of taps close together—a string of ricky-ticky-ticky-tacky-ticky-ticky taps."

After one season of watching Fred struggle week by week to get himself up for the radio show, Phyllis convinced him not to sign on for a second season. She thought it was just a bit too much, since Fred had to spend so much of his time in preparation for his motion-picture routines.

There were good things and there were bad things in that period of time. In September 1935, Fred and Phyllis received the shattering news from Ireland that Adele had lost twin boys at birth. Now she would never be able to have children.

"She wrote to me of her bitter disappointment and near despondency," Fred said in his autobiography.

When *Follow the Fleet* was finally in the can, Fred stayed close to home to await the arrival of his own baby. He was more nervous than he ever had been waiting to make a stage entrance or film a scene; he kept wanting her to check in at the hospital ahead of time.

"I hate hospitals!" Phyllis protested. "Don't worry; I'll know in plenty of time. I wouldn't think of going down there *one second* earlier than I have to."

On the morning of January 21, sure enough, she woke him up and told him she was ready. He drove from the house to Good Samaritan Hospital in eighteen minutes, got her checked in, and then began the old routine of pacing up and down that he had seen in a hundred movies.

In a half hour the nurse announced, "You're the pappy of a boy."

That was Fred, Jr.

He had begun to gather around him a small but select group of people as friends. He rarely went out on the town, if ever. Nor did he like big parties, the type Hollywood loved to throw. He liked intimate groups.

One day a shirtless man who reminded Phyllis of some kind of out-of-work bum appeared at the door of the house and asked for Fred. He told her he knew Fred's sister and had a letter of introduction from some English bookie.

It was David Niven, who had, indeed, a letter of introduction from Lord Graves, probably the only titled bookie on the island. Fred had dealt with Lord Graves, all right, and he asked the Hollywood newcomer in. It was the beginning, however inauspicious, of a fast friendship.

David Niven: "From these unpromising beginnings, a friendship grew which perhaps meant more to me than any other in Hollywood."

They were together frequently, on hunting trips, on fishing trips, on racetrack visits—as often as they could be together.

It was about this time that Phyllis suddenly spotted the property where she wanted to build a house. It was on Summit Drive in Beverly Hills. The air was a lot better up there than it was in the city, which was beginning to experience even in those early days the hint of what was to become the bane of all cities: smog. It was a four-acre plot on a steep part of the hill. John Boles had owned it but had never developed it.

It was a choice piece of real estate. The Spalding estate, with its orange groves, lay next to it, and then there was Pickfair, Mary Pickford's place, and below that, Charlie Chaplin's house. Work started immediately on the house, the swimming pool, and the tennis court.

Fred protested. "I don't like tennis. Everybody beats me."

Phyllis looked at him with amusement. "This house is not for us forever. It's for sale."

"Huh?"

She was a sharp woman with a flair for real estate. Within a short time, she had divided the property into two parts and sold the front house to William Wyler, the director who would later make *Wuthering Heights* and *Ben Hur*.

Hermes Pan: "She supervised the building of their home, saw to it that the plumbing got fixed when it broke down, ran the stables where he kept his racehorses, and handled all the business and social problems of the family."

And did so in a superb fashion.

It was at about this time, after the results of the box-office receipts of *A Damsel in Distress,* that Fred and Phyllis began talking together about retirement. They would travel across the country to Aiken, where Phyllis's uncle and aunt lived. Fred loved the racing stables in the area and watched the grooms working on the horses. He played golf there.

Why dance anymore?

"I'm thinking of retiring," he told Phyllis one day.

"Just because you had a good round of golf," she responded, "you're carried away with the idea of golf all the time. Just wait. If you have a bad round tomorrow, you'll have no idea of retiring."

The next day Fred shot a ninety.

Retire? Are you crazy?

After *The Story of Vernon and Irene Castle,* Fred and Phyllis took a long holiday from the motion-picture business. Of course, they headed first for London, then spent quite a while in Ireland before journeying to the Continent. Most of their time was spent in France and England.

This was 1939, and the Astaires could feel the threat of war in the air. In fact, London was nowhere near as gay as it had been before. In England the Astaires had lunch with Prince George and his wife, Marina—by then the duke and duchess of Kent. It was the last time Fred ever saw the duke. He was killed in an airplane accident during World War II on an official mission.

Fred's second child was born in March 1939. Before the birth, Fred mentioned once to Phyllis that it might be nice to have a girl to balance Fred, Jr., and Peter, Phyllis's son by her first marriage.

PHYLLIS: Oh, no. I don't want a girl!
FRED: Why not?
PHYLLIS: Oh, it would probably be an awful little brat like I was. No. No. I don't want a girl.
FRED: Come on. It wouldn't be so bad to have a little brat sister around the house.
PHYLLIS: Well, I'll think about it.

This time Fred was prepared for the arrival. He took Phyllis in hand and made her check into Good Samaritan early, in spite of her vehement protests and pleadings.

The timing was perfect. The next morning the Astaires had a little girl. They named her Ava—pronounced "Ah-Vah."

"I must be about the happiest fellow in the world," Fred said.

Happiness was a sometime thing. Adele refused to leave Ireland when the war broke out in Britain. Fred kept in constant touch with her, checking to make sure she was all right and trying to do anything he or Ann could do for the Cavendishes. Ann sent large parcels of dried California fruit to them as often as she could.

With the war now on full scale, Fred found it difficult to concentrate on the motion-picture business. He made several movies, however, but he was glad to do as much as he could— working with Phyllis—selling war bonds. In September 1942 the two of them toured the state of Ohio on a trip arranged by the Hollywood Victory Committee.

Huge crowds came out to see him. The people in charge of the tour tried to squeeze in too many extra appearances at the last minute, and the schedule was constantly up in the air.

There were so many people attracted by the name of Fred Astaire, Hugh ("Woo Woo") Herbert, and Ilona Massey that the traffic got to be a problem whenever they went. They were accompanied by state troopers, who pushed back the crowds so they could get through to the places where they were supposed to appear.

Fred made twenty to thirty appearances a day over a two-week period, some 350 altogether, in Columbus, Akron, Canton, Springfield, Mansfield, Zanesville, and so on to Cincinnati, Middletown, and Delaware.

In Cleveland, Fred sold a pair of his old tap shoes for $100,000 worth of bonds. A pair of his shoelaces went for $16,000.

It was an exhausting ordeal, but for a good cause. "Phyl and I found it all pretty good fun."

The second tour included a huge group of top stars, starting in Washington, D.C., and going all over the country. The group moved westward after a big appearance at Madison Square Garden in New York. All the stars would sleep in their private train and then were rushed back and forth by military escorts during the day.

The show was a tremendous success. Fred had a seven-minute song and dance with Kay Kyser's band. Phyllis stayed home but was apprised of the details every day in letters from Fred that related the events. The big tour ended up in San Francisco. Everybody was prepared for enormous crowds.

San Francisco was deserted. The group drove through the city from the railway station with no one watching. The punch line: Somebody had screwed up. San Francisco did not know that the group was arriving.

It took a lot of hard work to get a quick crowd assembled for the event. With radio announcements and newspaper stories, the show did finally go on, but the grand finale was the weakest part of the whole tour.

Fred then took part in a trip overseas with the USO—the United Service Organizations—to entertain the troops in France. They hit Paris just after Liberation Day. Fred was astonished to find automobiles all over town overturned and on fire. He found himself staring at three of them near a truck that had been blown up against the entrance of the Hotel Crillon, where he and Phyllis had stayed many times in the past.

They toured to the front, and then Fred returned to Paris, where he made a personal appearance before General Spaatz. He was exhausted when he finally got back home.

Then news came from Ireland that was very bad. Adele was at work with the American Red Cross, hundreds of miles away from home, when her husband Charles fell ill. She was unable to get a permit to cross the Irish Sea to Lismore, since the war was still raging. Charles was nursed by his own mother in his last days; he had been sick for some time, but it was a bitter blow to Adele not to be there with him.

Meanwhile, the Astaires had bought a ranch in the San Fernando Valley, where they spent their weekends and periods between pictures with the children.

Hermes Pan remembered: "I'd go over to the ranch, and Phyllis would be puttering around in dungarees, painting the fireplace or cooking or doing the dishes. After dinner Fred would generally fall asleep in front of the fire."

It was Pan who remembered one of the seldom repeated anecdotes about Fred and his excitable temperament.

One night, she said to him, "*You* do the dishes." He said, "Okay," and went into the kitchen. A moment later, we heard a terrible clatter. We rushed inside and found Fred breaking the dishes—one at a time. He said, "Never ask me to do dishes again." Ninety-nine wives out of a hundred would have blown their tops over that, but Phyllis just burst out laughing. Then she pitched in and helped break the rest of the dishes. She knew you could push Fred—but only up to a point. That's the kind of relationship it was.

By now Fred took months off every year to spend long vacations with his wife and children and to supervise his growing stable of racehorses. One of them, Triplicate, turned out to be a real winner. On June 1, 1945, Triplicate won the seventh and featured race of the day at Santa Anita. The following year, Triplicate came in sixth in a blanket finish at the Santa Anita Handicap, only two lengths behind in the best of the Santa Anita Handicap field of twenty-three runners.

He later won the San Juan Capistrano by five open lengths. But the big race was the Hollywood Gold Cup at Hollywood Park. In that, Triplicate won the race, coming from far back to beat Louis B. Mayer's Honeymoon by a neck at the wire.

After winning the Golden Gate Handicap for $75,000, he went on to win many more races in 1947 and 1948, and then he was retired to stud in Kentucky at seven.

Everything was going so well that Astaire was consistently described as one of the happiest people in Hollywood.

For a while.

Fred, Jr., enlisted in the air force on his eighteenth birthday, leaving a big void in family life back home on Summit Drive. It was while he was taking his training in Texas that Phyllis, sitting in the Astaires' box seat at Santa Anita, suddenly wanted to go home.

"I don't feel well. It's nothing. Just that dizziness."

"That dizziness" had been recurring, but no matter how much Fred insisted, he could not get her to a doctor.

One evening soon after that, Phyllis was unable to go to a dancing-class function of Ava's. A week later she made Fred call off a dinner appointment with Cole Porter and his wife, Linda. Finally, he got her to a doctor.

The physician took X rays and found a suspicious shadow on her lungs. The Astaires canceled a trip over Easter to visit Fred, Jr., in Texas. Instead, Phyllis went to the hospital for an operation.

At St. John's Hospital, on Good Friday, the operation was performed, successfully—but it was serious. Two of Fred's best friends—David Niven and Hermes Pan—were at his side sitting with him while Fred waited for the verdict.

The doctor appeared; he said she was doing pretty well. Actually, she was in serious condition, and it was not known if she would live through the night. However, in the morning she came out of it and seemed to be doing fine. The surgeons had removed a large part of one of her lungs.

After that she had a series of X-ray treatments. Fred was always at her side. Three months afterward, she seemed completely cured. The Astaires spent time at the ranch with the children.

Then, in August, she had to go back to St. John's for more surgery. The operation was a success, and she came home. This time she did not snap back. She lapsed into a coma and remained in it for several weeks. She died on September 13, 1954. It was lung cancer.

Things were never the same again for Fred Astaire.

At the time of this ordeal, Fred was just about to start a motion picture for Sam Engel at Twentieth Century-Fox. It was *Daddy Long Legs*.

Engel said:

The day after Phyllis's funeral, Fred sent for me. He was in a bad way—sort of in a daze. The week before, we had had a talk in which he said he couldn't go on with the picture. He then made me an offer that was unheard of in Hollywood. He wanted to pay all the expenses of the production out of his own pocket. I told him to forget it—that maybe God would intervene and Phyllis would pull through.

Well, I showed up at Fred's house the day after the funeral. He said, "Sam, what I told you last week still goes. The kids are shattered and I'm shattered. The worst thing is that Phyllis wanted me to do this picture. But I can't. The prospect of going to the studio and smiling is just impossible." I said, "Don't worry about it, Fred. If you feel the way you do, that's it. However, I think you'll be making the greatest mistake in your life if you don't go to work right now." Fred shook his head and said, "Sam, I just can't." So I said goodbye and left.

About eleven o'clock the next morning, as Engel was gloomily sitting in his office, Fred walked in. "I don't know if I can make it, Sam, but I'll try. I'm reporting for work."

Engel said:

It was a frightful ordeal for the poor man. He'd be dancing as if nothing had happened, and then he'd come over in a corner and talk to me. He'd say, "I don't know if Old Dad can make it," and tears would come to his eyes. I'd say, "It's okay. It's all right to cry." He'd say, "It's rough, Sam, real rough. Especially going home and she's not there." Then he'd talk about how Phyllis wanted him to make this picture, and he'd go back to work. When *Daddy Long Legs* was finally released, Fred was so good in it that I'm sure the audience never guessed his heart was breaking. His class emerged when he wrote me a letter saying, "Thanks for standing by Old Dad." It should have been the other way around.

Randolph Scott remembered those days:

After *Daddy Long Legs* was finished, Fred used to go to the cemetery and sit at Phyllis's grave for hours at a time. Like Sam Engel, we all felt that work was the best thing for him, and we talked him into doing *Funny Face* and *Silk Stockings* as soon as possible.

No, it was never really the same again for him.

PART THREE

The Renaissance Man
1939–87

Chapter Twelve

"Stepping Out with My Babies"

The Astaire-Rogers combination was at an end, even though the two of them would make one more picture together in 1949. The nine pictures they made in a period of six years, as Derek Conrad wrote in *Films and Filming* in 1959, "are perhaps representative of the true Astaire: uncomplicated routines suggesting momentary improvisation."

Conrad goes on to elaborate:

> His latest pictures [those made after the Astaire-Rogers period] are more formally choreographed and the routines are often tricked up against stylistic backgrounds. In his early films the success of most of his numbers was due to his completely informal approach played out against natural settings.

And those Art Deco sets, too.

Fred was a realist. He knew that his partnership with Ginger Rogers—against which each had fought bitterly with Berman through the years—had brought him international fame and had made both their names household words. He also was quite aware of the fact that when he had tried to wing it on his own—or pretty much on his own—in *Damsel in Distress,* he had bombed. Sure, the routines were good, but the picture wound up in the debit column, and not by any smidgeon, either.

What he wanted to be, a soloist, obviously wasn't in the cards for him. At least not yet. His stature, of course, always gave him a good "in" with the studios in Hollywood. Yet the next years were nomadic ones for him. He wandered from studio to studio, appearing with a variety of partners and he certainly made plenty of money.

He made three films for M-G-M for which he got $150,000

apiece, two for Columbia at $100,000, three for Paramount at the same rate, and another back at RKO, also at $100,000 plus a share of the profits.

It was M-G-M that reunited Astaire with a Cole Porter score in *Broadway Melody of 1940*. His dancing partner there was Eleanor Powell, a major talent the studio was nurturing. A long-legged female dynamo of a tap dancer in the machine-gun tradition, she almost overpowers him with her smashing runs up and down stairs, leaps over tables, and a lot of balancing on chairs. Somehow he seems to find it difficult to relate romantically to her, and although they sing two duets in the film, the performers rarely seem to touch one another.

One of their numbers is "Begin the Beguine," another weirdly structured Porter opus: AABACC, with the eerie length of 104 measures—almost three times the usual thirty-two! It is so long, in fact, that one segment, the second A, has been dropped, and the number is played at least two-thirds faster than the famous Artie Shaw rendition of it in the late thirties.

But the Astaire-Powell dance is a honey. It's done on a mirrored floor against a starry background. As the tempo changes, a vocal quartet sings, and Fred and Eleanor appear once more, this time in black and white, and build the number to a tremendous climax—tapping for what seems like an eternity without any accompaniment at all.

Fred even dances a short duet with George Murphy, "Please Don't Monkey with Broadway," a kind of retrospective on vaudeville. Murphy plays his show-biz partner.

From M-G-M, Fred went to Paramount where he made *Second Chorus* in 1940. The producer of this musical, which starred Paulette Goddard with Astaire, was Boris Morros. Later, when the United States got into the war, Morros entered the intelligence service and became an espionage agent, later writing a book entitled *My Years as a Counterspy*.

In the picture, directed by H. C. Potter, who had made the *Castle* opus at RKO, Fred spends most of his time arguing with Burgess Meredith rather than romancing Goddard, which would seem to be the main point of the story. But Goddard was definitely an inept dancer and singer, even though she had a great deal of sex appeal on the screen.

And so Fred supplies the bulk of the dancing and the singing to a marvelous backup band—Artie Shaw's! When Fred gets up and dances in front of the Artie Shaw orchestra in at least one of his numbers, he stands out as a soloist of the first order.

For doing this turkey—and turkey it was—Fred got the worst notices of his movie career. A "slaphazard picture," Bosley

Crowther of the *New York Times* called it—and that was the mildest of his comments. What was even worse, Ginger Rogers appeared during that same year in a tearjerker called *Kitty Foyle*, adapted from a Christopher Morley tearjerker. For her role she received an Academy Award! Fred was down that year; she was up. He sent her a one-word telegram: "OUCH!"

The next year, 1941, Fred was working for Columbia doing *You'll Never Get Rich* with Rita Hayworth. Hayworth was of course the daughter of Fred's old vaudeville friends, the Cansinsos. She was actually an overpowering beauty, and a pretty good dancer, too. Although Pearl Harbor was still in the future, the country was drifting into World War II. The "oomph" girl was the "in" type. Rita was definitely oomphy.

With music by Cole Porter, this picture is a kind of an advance recruiting poster for the war effort, with Fred as the prototypical serviceman, a sort of mental flashback to the character he played in *Follow the Fleet*. There's a recruiting dance in it, too, called the "March Militaire." There is also "The Wedding Cake March," a big extravaganza with gobs of girls, gobs of servicemen, and a giant wedding cake topped by a tank. Huh?

With the war coming on in full swing, Fred moved to Paramount, where Irving Berlin had been commissioned to write a score for *Holiday Inn*—no relation to the hotel chain, which did not even exist then. The idea was to pair Astaire with Paramount's singing star, Bing Crosby. And who better to direct but Mark Sandrich, who came over to Paramount for the picture.

The gimmick was to feature American holidays in song and dance, with each holiday getting a nod. Berlin surpassed himself on one song, something he more or less dashed off to fill in the Christmas spot. It was called "White Christmas," and it hit the national sensibility like a bolt from heaven. The royalties are still rolling in on that song; it has been said that Berlin could live a life of ease probably for about two hundred years on the money that tune alone made him.

Bing is the winner of the girl, Fred the loser, displaying to good effect his old friendly vulnerability. The big dance number keys nicely to the military situation that was crowding in; it's a Fourth of July number called "Say It with Firecrackers." This is a spectacular routine in which Fred's dancing sets off explosions on the dance floor as if his taps are torpedoes.

The same year, Fred was back at Columbia making *You Were Never Lovelier*, directed by William Seiter and starring Rita Hayworth for the second and last time with him. It had a Jerome Kern–Johnny Mercer score. Fred does the Shorty George with Hayworth in one sequence and a song and dance with her to the

Kern-Mercer song "I'm Old Fashioned." The routine for "You Were Never Lovelier" is reminiscent of early Astaire-Rogers—he in his white tie and tails, she in a white dress. But her legs are longer than Ginger's.

In the "I'm Old Fashioned" routine, Fred dances with Rita on a terrace, then in a garden, the music segueing from old-fashioned fox-trot to Latin American, after which they do whirls, then a walk into the crawls at the windup of the film. Johnny Mercer once described it as "one of those *nice* pictures." He meant one in which everybody dressed up. "Fred was always in tails going through French windows, dancing on the terrace. One of those pictures."

But not bad, not bad.

Back at the old studio, RKO, Fred made *The Sky's the Limit* in 1943. This was a military-oriented story about a pilot who has returned from the war against Japan. Fred is teamed with Joan Leslie. Music and lyrics were by Harold Arlen and Johnny Mercer. Robert Benchley appeared in one of his classic parodies of the boring after-dinner speaker.

The knockout dance in the picture is Fred's stunning solo "One for My Baby (and One More for the Road)." In a bar a miserable Fred tries to contemplate a world without his girlfriend. He sings the Arlen song with its Mercer lyrics and then begins a dance, building it to a rousing climax as he jumps up and around, breaking glasses, mirrors, and most of the decor of the bar before the end.

After bond sales, rallies, and a visit overseas to entertain the troops, Fred reappeared on the screen in *Yolanda and the Thief* for M-G-M, with producer Arthur Freed supplying the lyrics for the songs and Harry Warren the music. Vincent Minelli directed. This one was in glowing Technicolor, with Fred's partner Lucille Bremer, a young girl who has a Guardian Angel. The Angel is played by reformed comedian Leon Errol, who eventually tries to reform Fred the thief. There is a nice dream sequence in this one filmed in color—a kind of finalizing of the color dream sequence that never came off in *Carefree*.

Fred reprised at M-G-M the following year with a "prestige" picture, *The Ziegfeld Follies,* a million-dollar movie. The casting included Lucille Ball, Lucille Bremer, Judy Garland, Kathryn Grayson, Lena Horne, and—oops!—Gene Kelly. William Powell incarnated Ziegfeld.

Billed as "the most sumptuous Technicolor revue in screen history," the picture was crammed with talent, with songs, and with dances. Fred dreams up one of his most marvelous duets for "Limehouse Blues," which he dances with Bremer. It is a masterpiece of subtlety and timing. He even looks good in Chinese. He later appears with Kelly singing and dancing to an old song Fred originally did on Broadway, "The Babbitt and the Bromide." This is the only film, sadly, in which Astaire and Kelly ever dance together. Except, of course, for a brief fling years later in a segment of *That's Entertainment.*

The picture itself? It became a studio legend that the thing was known in-house as *Ziegfeld's Folly,* and the critics were about on the same wavelength when they reviewed it.

Fred then went to Paramount to join Bing Crosby in a picture called *Blue Skies.* It was to be directed by Mark Sandrich, with a score by Irving Berlin. Paul Draper was cast to costar with Bing but couldn't seem to get the part together because of a bad stammer. Sandrich began to worry. He thought of replacing Draper with Fred. He suggested this to Bing, but nothing was done. Suddenly, and sadly, Sandrich suffered a fatal heart attack, and Sol C. Siegel replaced him. When it became evident that Draper was not going to work out, Bing and Siegel called in Fred.

He obliged and made a good costar for Bing. The picture includes one of Fred's most memorable routines, "Puttin' on the Ritz." This is a technologically marvelous split-screen deal that shows a whole background filled with Fred Astaires—not fakes but the real thing!—tap dancing with his marvelous easy precision. It's sensational even in stills. To many fans, "Puttin' on the Ritz" is *the* Fred Astaire number.

There's also an Astaire-Crosby duet entitled "A Couple of Song and Dance Men," a tribute to the old burlesque and music-hall days. It's a showstopper, too.

Crosby impressed Fred with his professionalism. "He's a wonderful performer. His dancing tickles me to death. But if I said he was a good dancer, it would be the same as Bing calling me a good singer."

It was after *Blue Skies* was wrapped that Fred threatened to retire. Officially, he did retire. Except that he came out of retirement quite soon after that to do *Easter Parade,* again by Irving Berlin, in which he played opposite Judy Garland. This project, too, developed from a backstage "emergency." Gene Kelly was slated for the lead role but broke his ankle in a touch-football game on the grounds of his home. With Gene's blessing, Fred was urged to come in. And so in November 1947 Fred was back at work.

This M-G-M musical had everything: lavish production against the lush background of the theater—agents, stage-door Johnnies, songs, acts, dances. Irving Berlin supplied "A Couple of Swells" for Fred and Judy, which they sing dressed up as a couple of tramps pretending to be on their way to tea at the Vanderbilts'.

Fred had trouble with his tramp costume and kept trying new versions that he showed to Judy Garland, asking hesitantly, "Is this too much?"

Judy was amused, and when she finally got her own outfit worked up, she went over to Fred's trailer in full clownish costume and makeup and knocked on the door. Fred came to the door, opened it, and looked out in astonishment.

"Is this too much?" Judy asked him with a grin.

The big Easter Parade that winds up the picture is the nut of the show, of course. The parade was so popular when the picture opened in London that a similar kind of parade was initiated in Hyde Park!

Easter Parade was so good, and Judy and Fred did so well together, that M-G-M proposed a new property for them. This was titled *You Made Me Love You,* after Judy's marvelous song to Clark Gable. The story, written by Betty Comden and Adolph Green, concerns a dance team that splits up so the woman can become a dramatic actress. Does that stir up memories?

Once again, it was to emerge in a slightly different fashion than intended. Judy Garland was beginning to fall apart emotionally again. She was on heavy medication. She kept coming in late, then failed to appear at all. Her physician warned the studio of trouble if she was pushed too hard. There was no way out but to replace her by—are you ready for this?—Ginger Rogers.

Fred was dismayed. Not again!

And yet it was again. Songs had to be changed. The title itself was changed to *The Barkleys of Broadway,* the theory being that without Judy Garland, "You Made Me Love You" meant nothing except to point up her absence. It's a solid picture. Fred and Ginger have one number—a rehearsal tap routine called "Bouncin' the Blues"—and it has the old magic. So does a reprise of "They Can't Take That Away from Me" from *Shall We Dance.*

Best, though, is a solo Fred worked out with Hermes Pan, this one set in a shoe shop. "Shoes without Wings" is one of the most advanced dance routines of its time. The idea was originally Hermes Pan's, stolen from *The Sorcerer's Apprentice,* of course. The shoe salesman is the apprentice, and all the shoes come to life in the shop. In the end he is forced to shoot them all one by one or beat them to death in any way he can.

The Astaire-Rogers matchup in the show was fine, but somehow it never did come up to the expectations of the public that remembered them as the golden team of the thirties. One thing about the past: It was never really as good as *it seems to be.*

In 1950, in *Three Little Words,* Fred played Bert Kalmar, the songwriter whom Fred and Adele had known and admired years before. "We used to stand in the wings and watch Jessie and Bert with thrilled envy, wondering if we could equal their finesse and reach their headline billing," Fred wrote. M-G-M made the picture, casting Red Skelton as Harry Ruby, Kalmar's musical partner. Vera-Ellen turned out to be a good match for Fred—her height and slimness matched Fred's. "Mr. and Mrs. Hoofer at Home" is almost a perfect duet of its type.

Hermes Pan worked very closely with Fred on this film, and some experts feel that in this picture he was much more in control of the choreography than usual. The dance numbers are great, one a trio with Fred, Red, and Vera-Ellen doing "Nevertheless" after Red Skeleton bangs it out on the piano. "Thinking of You," another of the great Kalmar-Ruby songs of the past, provides another fine duet.

In 1950, Fred also made *Let's Dance*, costarred with Betty Hutton. "The volcanic Miss Hutton and the shy Astaire are like Garbo and Durante together," one critic complained. Their two styles of dancing were simply incompatible. Nevertheless, a Fred Astaire solo "Jack and the Beanstalk" is a showstopper, particularly when he creates a beanstalk out of a rolled-up newspaper—the same nightclub act that Orson Bean always did so well.

The following year Fred did *Royal Wedding,* set in 1947 during the wedding of Princess Elizabeth and Prince Philip. Alan Jay Lerner was in Hollywood at that time and supplied the lyrics to the songs by Burton Lane—and most of the script. The big bombshell number in this film is the gimmicked routine in which Fred dances on the walls and then the ceiling of his room. In this trick dance, done to "You're All the World to Me," the camera is mounted to a rotating room so that Fred seems to be on the floor, on the walls, on the ceiling, and so on down to the floor again as the room and camera are turned completely over once.

M-G-M must have had plenty of mechanical sets, because a similar gimmick is worked in the dance number Jane Powell and Fred do on board a ship, with the deck beginning to toss in a storm. To film it, the floor was simply moved about as they fell and recovered their balance. In another novelty duet Fred and Jane sing "How Could You Believe Me When I Said I Love You When You Know I've Been a Liar All My Life," purportedly the longest song title ever written. The finale is a production number unusual for Fred Astaire—"I Left My Hat in Haiti," a lavish production number with eighty chorus girls behind him!

The Belle of New York, another M-G-M picture, is about a free-living bachelor who woos a Salvation Army girl—as in *Guys and Dolls*—and wins her. Vera-Ellen costarred. It is a period piece set around the turn of the century and gives Fred a chance to wear his top hat, white tie, and tails quite naturally. The big gimmick routine is the one he does to "Seeing's Believing" in which he solos in the air over the city after he discovers he can stride across the sky at will. Another solo, "I Wanna Be a Dancin' Man," is a beaut. He also does a nice ice-skating dance to "Oops" with Vera-Ellen.

Jack Buchanan, an English dancer often called the "British Fred Astaire," joined Fred and Cyd Charisse to remake one of Fred's earlier successes on Broadway, *The Band Wagon*. The plot was all thrown out, along with all of the songs except for five. With new music by Howard Dietz and Arthur Schwartz, this version contained a lot of good songs and routines.

Hermes Pan once made an observation about Fred's dancing partners. "Except for the times Fred worked with real professional dancers like Cyd Charisse, it was a twenty-five-year war." Ballet trained, Charisse came to the movie with plenty of credentials. Before she was selected for the role, Fred did some reconnoitering, dropping by the set where she was doing a dance routine under the direction of Pan.

Charisse recalled: He came in nonchalantly, pretending he was just visiting his old friend. . . . I could see that he was there to size me up—for size. . . . Even though we had danced in the same number together . . . when we did *Ziegfeld Follies* he wanted to make sure, I guess, that I hadn't grown any. . . . He did it very subtly, very tactfully. Then he just smiled and strolled out.

And she got the part.

"Dancing in the Dark" is typically a fine example of their work together. So is "Girl Hunt Ballet," a marvelous duet for which Fred has been praised many times. Incidentally, Michael Kidd choreographed the dances in the picture. Buchanan and Fred dance together to "I Guess I'll Have to Change My Plan," designed in a way to show, presumably, how alike they are. Both are dressed in the usual tails and carry canes.

Shortly after finishing *The Band Wagon*, Phyllis died, and it was only after Fred thought it out that he returned to do his scheduled film *Daddy Long Legs* for Twentieth Century-Fox. In this one he has a new partner, Leslie Caron, a classical ballet dancer from France. The "dream dance" was choreographed by Roland Petit, flown over to Hollywood and paid a large sum of money for a ballet that takes up only fifteen minutes of the film. The picture was photographed in a new wide-screen process—Cinemascope. Fred liked the width of the screen and made full use of it in his routines. One of the strange audience fallouts after the picture opened was that some purists were annoyed at the pairing off of Fred Astaire and Leslie Caron. He was too old for her!

Another reprise followed—Fred's old favorite, *Funny Face*. This one costarred him with Audrey Hepburn and Kay Thompson. Instead of using the Paramount lot, the picture was shot on location in Paris. The filming and the special effects are very good. There is a stunning split-screen routine for "Bonjour Paris" that has Astaire, Hepburn, and Thompson exploring Paris together side by side on a huge wide screen.

Later, in the deep red of a darkroom, Fred sings "Funny Face" while developing a photograph of Audrey Hepburn. There is a windup sequence of Thompson and Astaire singing and dancing "Clap Yo' Hands" at an existentialist meeting.

At M-G-M, Fred then made *Silk Stockings*, the hit Broadway musical with songs by Cole Porter, for Rouben Mamoulian. In this musical remake of the play *Ninotchka*, Fred wins over the Russian miss and converts her to the American way. Cyd Charisse costarred, playing the Russian girl. Fred was now fifty-seven years old, and he was working on his thirtieth film.

Interestingly enough, Eugene Loring, the choreographer for the stage version of the musical, was asked to work on the film, as well. Loring had done *Funny Face* and *Yolanda and the Thief* with Fred. "I prefer *not* to choreograph for Astaire again," Loring told M-G-M in no uncertain terms. "By that I mean it's hard to create for him and get something new and fresh that also pleases him. He's very set in his ways."

Fred called in Hermes Pan. They were used to each other. Pan didn't think Fred was "too set in his ways." "Fated to Be Mated" is an exceptionally good duet between Fred and Cyd. It has a bunch of jumps and lifts and other acrobatics that are amazing to see when one considers Astaire's age at the time. Apparently Hermes Pan, who choreographed the dance almost in its entirety, was "having one on" with those fans who thought Fred might be "too old for the girls."

One of the best gags in the movie is "The Ritz Roll and Rock." The idea is to get some comedy out of the sight of Fred Astaire doing a rock-and-roll number. The first person to object—and vehemently—was Cole Porter.

"I don't know how to write a rock-and-roll song!" he cried in consternation. But after studying the genre a bit, he decided to play it tongue and cheek—as he always played everything, anyway—and worked out an idea. He came up with the concept of what would happen to rock and roll if it were taken over by the "swells," as he put it. Of course this routine would feature Fred doing the number in the traditional tails, but as a satiric parody.

Now Fred was objecting. "I haven't been in tails for two pictures! The idea's passé! Can't I—?"

He thought it over a bit and decided—why not?

In the end he sings the number a little bit too sarcastically. "It wasn't a great song to begin with, but it didn't have to be *that* bad. . . . I overdid, overplayed, it." He was not happy with his dance, either. Besides, nothing he or Cole Porter did would stop the onslaught of rock and roll. This is what really depressed him.

"What's happened to music, anyway?" he asked in an interview about the "new" rock-and-roll phenomenon. "The songs you hear pouring out of radio and jukeboxes sound sick. What's happened? Is there some kind of contest to see who can write the ugliest songs? There's just a terrible sameness to this junk on the air."

At the end of this dance—the total collapse of all the principals, including a chorus dressed just like Fred—Fred falls on the ground, his hat rolls off, and, with savage glee, he takes steady aim at it nearby and smashes it flat—a somehow fitting end to this last filmed dance in a major musical.

Major, because *Finian's Rainbow* is now known throughout the industry as "Coppola's Disaster." Fred himself has called it his "biggest disappointment." "The bulk of what passes for choreography in this film must be credited to Coppola," wrote John Mueller in his book *Astaire Dancing*.

Hermes Pan was hired to work on the film at the early insistence of Fred Astaire, who was not sure what he was getting into when he signed the contract.

"I know nothing about dancing," Coppola claimed, but as the worked progressed, he let it be known that he found Pan's work "aybsmal." After a brief encounter, Coppola fired Pan halfway through the picture.

He then improvised all the dances as he went along. Fred once said that he had tried to make several suggestions to Coppola, but they were all ignored.

Pan has called Coppola "a real pain. . . . He knew very little about dancing and musicals. He would interfere with my work and even with Fred's. . . . Those schoolboys who studied at UCLA think they're geniuses, but there is a lot they don't understand."

Probably the less said about the film the better. It's best to pretend Fred's last dance was in *Silk Stockings*.

Chapter Thirteen

Man of Many Top Hats

B y the time Fred Astaire had finished making the motion picture *Silk Stockings,* he had virtually initiated, developed, and conquered on the highest level two completely different professional careers. With his sister Adele he had become the toast of two continents as a musical-comedy star. And on his own he had revolutionized the concept of dance in the film industry and became a worldwide and generally acknowledged superstar of dance.

Two solid careers, and complete master of both! Each would be an amazing achievement for any individual.

For Fred Astaire it was only the beginning. This remarkable man had even then risen to the top of at least two *other* careers— writing and singing—and was now waiting to step into yet *another* career in which he was to make his mark in the fifth and sixth decades of his life. To understand more clearly exactly what he accomplished in each, let's take the careers one by one to see what he did to conquer them.

These careers encompass, in addition to stage success and film-dancing success, the following: "straight" dramatic acting, television performance, professional songwriting, vocal recording, management of a successful chain of dance schools, and autobiographical writing.

He was a man who could wear—and did—many hats, and what is even more exceptional, every hat this man wore was a *top* hat!

Astaire as "Straight" Dramatic Actor

Fred's dramatic acting career really started in 1957 when Stanley Kramer read a novel by Nevil Shute entitled *On the Beach* about the annihilation of mankind in a nuclear war. He quickly secured the film rights and began to work with John Paxton on a screenplay. Sure, the picture had a message, but it was a message that needed articulating dramatically.

Most of the roles fell into place easily: Gregory Peck as the American submarine commander, Ava Gardner as the loose and lovely lady, Anthony Perkins as the embittered naval officer. The question was, who would play the alcoholic English scientist? It was a key role, since it is that man—Julian Osborn—who delivers the film's message after being castigated by a military man for being one of the scientists who had invented the atom bomb:

Every man who ever worked on this thing told you what would happen. The scientists signed petition after petition. But nobody listened. There *was* a choice. It was to build the bombs and use them. Or hope the United States and the Soviet Union and the rest of us would find some way to go on living.

And the final word:

The background radiation in this very room is nine times what it was a year ago. Don't you know that? Nine times! We're all doomed, you know. The whole silly, pathetic lot of us! Doomed by the air we are about to breathe. We haven't got a chance!

Serious stuff. Lines that must be delivered by a seasoned actor. Someone who could convince an audience.

The story goes that Kramer's wife was watching a late show one night on television with him and suddenly pointed to the screen where Fred Astaire was performing:

"There's your scientist."

Kramer was unamused. Then he took another hard look at the screen. He watched. Finally, he said, "By God, you're right!"

Fred was curious when Kramer came to him and asked him to join the cast. "Why me? You've got a world of talent to choose from."

"You've got something most actors don't have, Fred. Integrity. It shines out of you."

Shot in 1959 in Melbourne, Australia, the work was a welcome relief to Fred, whose home was pretty deserted then, with all the kids away. His deeply ingrained dramatic ability stood him in good stead, and his light, seemingly effortless manner is in welcome contrast to Peck's grimness, Perkins's self-hatred, and Gardner's moroseness. Having played plenty of drunks in his long career, he does it gracefully without having to overdo it. Because he was an active sports enthusiast, he brings to the role of this racing enthusiast the proper amount of authenticity as he prepares himself for his last race, which he ends in a suicidal auto crash. Stanley Kramer remembered Astaire's work on the picture with real affection and admiration at his professionalism.

You'd think that Fred had been playing serious drama all his life. He breaks your heart. We had to get rid of any signs that this was Fred Astaire, the dancer, and I even thought of putting weights in his shoes to eliminate that jaunty Astaire walk. But I didn't have to do anything. He worked it all out on his own—even to mussing the hair of his toupee to get rid of the sleek look of 'The Hoofer,' as he calls himself.

Bosley Crowther thought Fred's performance was "amazing" and said that he felt Fred "conveyed in his self-effacing manner a piercing sense of the irony of his trade."

"Astaire's work is not only reminiscent of but compares favorably to an Alec Guiness performance," wrote Arthur Knight.

Newsweek: "Astaire has never performed better."

Once the die was cast, the field of straight film drama opened up for him, and he did *The Pleasure of His Company* in 1961, an updating by Samuel Taylor of his stage play. Fred plays the playboy father who suddenly reappears for his daughter's wedding. Debbie Reynolds is his daughter; Lilli Palmer, his former wife. His light comedy is buoyant and stimulating. It's fluff, but delightful fluff.

Next came *The Notorious Landlady* in 1962, a comedy-mystery thriller coauthored by Blake Edwards. Jack Lemmon plays a British diplomat and Kim Novak a murder suspect. Fred is Lemmon's boss. The action takes place in Britain, and the dialogue is suitably light and bouncy. The critic on *The New Yorker* called it "a picture that is entertaining and exciting, often simultaneously. I don't see how anyone could help but have a good time watching it."

In *Midas Run* (1969), Fred is a veteran British secret-service officer who fails to attain a deserved knighthood and goes bad, hijacking a gold shipment worth fifteen million dollars. Richard Crenna and Anne Heywood join him, as does the solid British actor Ralph Richardson. Fred holds his own.

In putting together the film clips that were to make up *That's Entertainment,* Jack Haley, Jr., the son of *The Wizard of Oz*'s tin woodsman, got Gene Kelly and Fred Astaire to comment on some of the clips in the picture. In a reprise of that movie, *That's*

Entertainment Part II, the two veteran dancers were again signed to do commentaries and also to sing original songs together. Fred had insisted on a clause in the contract specifying "no dancing."

At the rehearsal the two dancers were learning the lyrics of a song written by Saul Chaplin, the associate producer. Fred turned to Gene at one point and said: "Gene, don't you think we can do sixteen bars of dancing here?"

Chaplin: "I just sat at the piano and stared straight ahead, hoping against hope that he wouldn't change his mind. And he didn't. In the film there are three or four scenes where they dance. And it was Fred's suggestion."

They are the high spots of the picture.

Jack Haley, Jr.:

I think my father said it best. He said film is timeless. He said if you take Fred Astaire and Eleanor Powell dancing to "Begin the Beguine," it's not dated. Excellence doesn't date, and that's an excellent number. People respond to excellence. They know that's good dancing; they know that's good music. So what if it is in black and white and it's forty years old? It doesn't matter. It's exciting and people appreciate it.

In 1974, Fred joined the cast of a high-budget "disaster" picture, *The Towering Inferno,* playing a con man caught up in a fire that destroys the world's tallest skyscraper. For that he was nominated—for the first time!—for an Academy Award. Sadly, he didn't win. But in a way it bears out the criticism of many reviewers and students of motion pictures that the awards are canted *away* from comedy and *toward* heavy message drama.

There were a couple of lesser efforts during those years: *The Amazing Dobermans* in 1976, with James Franciscus and Barbara Eden; *Un Taxi Mauve* (The Purple Taxi) in 1977, with Charlotte Rampling, Philippe Noiret, and Peter Ustinov; and *Ghost Story* in 1981, with Melvyn Douglas, Douglas Fairbanks, Jr., John Houseman, and Patricia Neal.

Anyone would have been happy to have lived *that* career alone!

Astaire as a Television Performer

As far back as 1955, Fred had appeared on Ed Sullivan's variety show to plug *Daddy Long Legs,* and in 1957 he appeared in a *General Electric Theater* play entitled "Imp on a Cobweb Leash." Beginning in 1958, he initiated what would be four television specials involving songs and dances—his breakthrough on the live television medium. Barrie Chase was his dancing partner. She had worked in *Silk Stockings* and had danced on skates with the Sonja Henie troupe. She was the daughter of novelist and screenwriter Borden Chase.

The four shows were blockbusters of their kind. The first was called *An Evening with Fred Astaire* (1958), the second *Astaire Time* (1960), the third *Hollywood Palace* (1966), and the fourth *The Fred Astaire Show* (1968).

Hermes Pan did three of these with Fred. David Rose remembered the two of them working together:

> I would walk into a rehearsal, and there would be dead silence for five minutes, with Fred and Hermes Pan just staring at each other. Then Hermes would say to Fred that he had the answer to their problem. He would step off on the left foot instead of the right. They had been debating for fifteen minutes which foot to step out on. Every step he took just had to be accounted for.

It was Fred's first "live" show—other than his hundreds of Broadway appearances—but if he was nervous, it did not show. The first of the four specials won nine Emmy Awards, including one for Fred as best actor! On its initial broadcast, the special was rated at a share of 18.9 percent of the audience; on its rebroadcast, January 1959, it achieved 26.2 percent! Better in retrospect?

He continued to appear in dramatic roles in various television anthology series, and even on some series shows like *Dr. Kildare*. Then, in 1969, he became a more or less featured player on *It Takes a Thief*, an update of the novel and movie *To Catch a Thief*. In it he played Alistair Mundy, the father of the series's hero, Robert Wagner.

He worked in five episodes: "It Takes a Thief," "The Great Casino Caper," "Three Virgins of Rome," "The Second Time Around," and "An Evening with Alistair Mundy."

As late as 1983 he made a television movie entitled *The Man in the Santa Claus Suit* in which he played at least six roles: a cabby, a New York cop, a jeweler, a floorwalker, a hot-dog-stand owner, and Santa Claus himself.

Again, any individual would have been proud of that television career by itself.

Astaire as Professional Songwriter

From the very beginning of his show-business days, Fred had always wanted to write songs. "I'm a frustrated songwriter," he once said, "and I would like to have written a musical-comedy score. But that's just about the only thing I didn't get done."

Even if he failed to achieve that goal, he did manage to write and publish a number of songs. In the long run, his most successful was "I'm Building up to an Awful Let-down," which he wrote in 1936, at the height of is fame as half the Astaire-Rogers team. That one had help from the prolific and proficient Johnny Mercer, who supplied the lyrics. It was used in the London stage show *Rise and Shine* and was sung by Bonnie Hale and Jack Whiting (Margaret Whiting's father).

Second in popularity, probably, was "Just Like Taking Candy from a Baby," which he wrote in 1940. This one had lyrics by Gladys Shelley.

Actually, his first song appeared in 1924, when he was working his way up the Broadway ladder. Called "You're Such a Lot," it had lyrics by Austin Melford and was sung in *The Co-Optimists* in London by Phyllis Monkman and Austin Melford.

After that he wrote "Tappin' the Time," with lyrics by Jock Whitney—that's right, *the* Jock Whitney, a close and good friend of Fred's in his Broadway days—and Jim Altemus. It appeared in *Shake Your Feet* in London, sung by Joyce Barbour.

A 1930 song with lyrics by Johnny Mercer and composed with Richard Myers, "More and More," was sung by Odette Myrtil in the Boston production of *Tattle Tales*. For the 1944 film *The Ziegfeld Follies,* Fred wrote "If Swing Goes, I Go Too." He sang it in the film, but the number was cut.

In 1962 he wrote three songs: "Girls Like You," with Tommy Wolf and with lyrics by Fred and Wolf; "I Love Everybody But You," with lyrics by his daughter, Ava, and himself; and "You Worry Me," for which he did both words and music.

Again, not a bad score for anyone in the music business.

Astaire as a Recording Star

Although everyone thought and thinks of Fred Astaire as a dancer and actor, he was also a consummate singer—as anyone can attest who watches any one of his musical films. Since 1923 his voice has appeared on records. In that year he debuted on a Monmouth-Evergreen disc, one of those old 78 rpm releases: "The Whichness of the Whatness" appeared on one side, "Oh, Gee! Oh, Gosh!" on the flip. On both sides he was teamed with Adele.

In 1926 he did two discs. One contained "Fascinating Rhythm," with Adele, and "The Half of It, Dearie, Blues" on the flip—accompanied on both by George Gershwin! The same trio made "Hang on to Me" and "I'd Rather Charleston," both from *Lady, Be Good!*

Singles were issued throughout his performing years. Later, when LPs came in, there were collections of those singles previously released and new "soundtrack" recordings of new movies and television specials. (A full list is included in the discography at the back of the book.)

Fred Astaire's achievements as a singer were of major importance to the pop music industry. He was a superb and vastly influential vocalist, one who had a tremendous effect on many other singers, including even the long-lasting and versatile Frank Sinatra.

Not to hear Fred talk about it, though. Once asked for his opinion of his singing voice, he responded:

> Lousy! Well, not too bad, I suppose. I'm not a particular fan of my own singing voice. I think the main reason I can be satisfied with it is that composers have liked the way I do their songs. But I'd have been broke if I had tried to be a singer alone.

Oh? Many people would disagree with that estimate. For he had the quality of making the words in a song come to life—making their meaning more important than most other singers could, or did. It has been pointed out what when the Smithsonian Institution's authoritative seven-LP anthology *American Popular Song* was compiled in 1984, the editors included nine Astaire records—compared to five each for Tony Bennett, Ella Fitzgerald, Judy Garland, and Frank Sinatra.

In turn, it should be remembered that a remarkable number of major American popular songs were written for and introduced by Fred Astaire, including, of course, "Night and Day," "Cheek to Cheek," "A Fine Romance," and "They Can't Take That Away from Me." Both George Gershwin and Irving Berlin considered him the ideal male interpreter of their music—in spite of George's petulant letter about *Shall We Dance.*

Another career no recording artist would sneeze at.

Astaire as Business Manager

In one of his recurring periods of frustration with the motion-picture business—this one occurred in 1946—Fred decided to put his remarkable creative talents to work teaching others how to dance the way he did. And why not make a little money at the same time?

As he told a reporter from *Time* magazine, "There comes a day when people begin to say, 'Why doesn't that old duffer retire?' I want to get out while they're still saying that Astaire is a hell of a dancer."

And get out he did—temporarily—to Manhattan, where he had gotten his own start with his sister a few years before. The idea was to open a dance school along the lines of the monumentally successful Arthur Murray dance studios. Naturally Fred was not about to supervise every individual dance student, but he planned to run the enterprise and keep a tight control over the teachers he hired.

For this venture Fred looked up an old friend, Charles Casanave, and together the pair of them worked out the details. Fred would put up $250,000–$300,000 to get the venture off the ground. Once the first school succeeded, they would open another branch in another city. He said he hoped to gross a million dollars in Manhattan alone the first year. And this man used to be called "Moaning Minnie"?

The decor of the place was to be modern, in good taste. There would be deep red carpets—at least in the reception room and certainly not on the dance floors!—blue-green walls, and yellow and red-covered furniture.

For seventy dollars for a ten-hour course, Fred was going to teach all comers, regardless of qualifications, to dance just like Fred Astaire. For the opening of the studio, which proved to be March 7, 1947, Fred choreographed a brand-new dance, "The Astaire." Actually, instead of leaping over furniture and tap dancing on tables, the step resembled the old "shag," in which the performer just jumped from one foot to another, as *Time* said, like a dog "trying to shake water from its ears."

Fred's promises to himself and to the venture with Casanave did not quite work out the way the partners had planned. By the end of the year, Fred was back in the movies, filling in for Gene Kelly, who had broken his ankle; Fred never did return to full-time operation of the dance school.

Nevertheless, after a shaky beginning, the school did succeed, with branches opening all over the country—indeed, the world. And soon enough, presumably everyone who wanted to—and had seventy bucks—could dance just like Fred Astaire.

In the 1960s, for example, there were 110 of these studios in the United States, Canada, and Mexico alone.

Another career no one would be ashamed of having launched.

Astaire as Autobiographical Author

By the end of the 1950s Fred decided that his life was pretty much behind him and that it was time to take a look at it from an impersonal point of view. He had been offered contracts to do his life story—or to have a "ghost" do it for him—but Fred had turned these deals down. What was the point of somebody else doing the story of *your* life?

But he did enlist the help of Cameron Shipp, a veteran studio publicist who knew his way around newspapers, magazines, and the book business and who had done the life stories of various entertainment "personalities" like Mack Sennett, Lionel Barrymore, and Billie Burke.

It was an upside-down collaboration. The professional writer usually writes it up, and the personality tones it down or straightens out the details. In this case, Fred did the preliminary draft—that is, *he* wrote the thing—and Shipp copyedited it.

As a matter of fact, Fred didn't even use a typewriter. He did the whole book longhand and had someone else type it up. Entitled *Steps in Time*—Noel Coward suggested it to him years before—it succeeded admirably. Even the critics liked it, quite probably because of its integrity and authenticity. It was obvious that Fred wrote it: The wording, the attitude, the amiability was all Fred Astaire.

Even *The New Yorker,* which either creams anything a Hollywood celebrity does or ignores it totally, liked it. Of course Fred to them was still a Manhattanite.

The book made the best-seller list and stayed there for some months.

Any author would be happy to accept *that* as a monument to a life work in the word business!

Chapter Fourteen

Life with Robyn

Even after his last dance movie, Fred kept himself in perfect physical shape, keeping in training with golf, shooting in the usual low eighties, playing a little tennis, and going fishing and sometimes skiing.

Just as he did in his early years, he rarely deviated from his base weight of 135. He continued on his ascetic diet, eating little more than an egg for breakfast, a light lunch, and a light dinner. Of course, in the days when he was creating new dance steps, he would routinely drop from fifteen to twenty pounds per picture, but would then gain it back when the picture was through. He never went on any fad "diets"; his body seemed to take care of itself, mostly since he never abused it by overeating or overdrinking.

In his eighties, he continued to eat lightly, smoked a bit and seldom drank. For him, one cocktail before a dinner party would be par for the course; two highballs afterward was for him almost a binge. He used to play gin rummy or bridge at night, and then he would go to bed early.

His mother Ann had died in 1975, after living part-time with him and his family in California and then in an apartment in New York City. She had lived a fine old life and had been able to see the fantastic achievements of her son and her daughter.

Adele had finally gotten over the shock of her husband's death during World War II and had moved back to the United States, where she married Kingman Douglass. He owned a place called Mount Gordon Farm in Middleburg, Virginia.

Fred continued to visit her; she was healthy and up and around, but she was getting older, and when she reached her eighties, she seemed to him to begin to deteriorate a bit.

Fred, Jr., was working here and there; he had, in fact, served a technical stint on the motion picture *On the Beach* and was continuing in that fashion. Married, he had left the old homesite. Ava was around and about.

The Blue Valley Ranch, Fred's horse-breeding farm in the San Fernando Valley, was coming along fine. Fred continued to enjoy going to the races. It was at one of them that he met a young jockey named Robyn Smith.

He had resisted the idea of marrying again; he and Phyllis had had so much together that anyone else in his life would have been redundant. When he had done his television specials with Barrie Chase, there had been a lot of talk about the two of them. But there was never *romance* there. "I wasn't even *thinking* about it," Fred once said.

But now, in 1980, he was beginning to feel a bit different about a remarriage. When he sounded out those closest to him, they were absolutely adamant *against* any new liaison.

And yet . . .

His kids were against it. Adele in particular was terribly upset over the idea of Fred's second marriage. Why? She had married again and had enjoyed two full married lives. She didn't know why, but it just *seemed* wrong. It was hard for her to change her ideas now.

In spite of the family, Fred married Robyn on June 24, 1980, at his home in Beverly Hills. She was thirty-seven; he was eighty-one. This shook up a lot of people: obviously the woman was nothing more than a gold digger after the old man's millions. And yet they were wrong.

Hermes Pan was as close to Fred as anyone, and he had known Phyllis very well.

"Robyn proved all the gossips and critics wrong—she proved to be a devoted and loving wife, constantly attentive to Fred," Pan said.

During the year following his marriage to Robyn, Fred became very worried about Adele. She was now beginning to go downhill rapidly. And, of course, she had been dead set against Fred's marriage; they had argued a lot about that. This did not sit well with her. With Robyn, Fred visited her in the winter of 1981 for the Christmas holidays.

Their visit tended to get things on a friendlier basis. Nevertheless, a month after they had left, Adele died of a stroke. Fred got the news when he was doing the movie *Ghost Story* on location in New York State.

"I can't believe it," he said. "It seems like yesterday that Delly and I were playing vaudeville together."

At this point, with the anxieties of mortality heavy on him, Fred persuaded Robyn to give up horse racing—which she had continued after their marriage, riding at Saratoga.

"I loved riding," Robyn admitted. "But I loved Fred more. And I couldn't have both."

She gave it up.

Even Fred was beginning to feel a little exhausted by all the work he was doing. He laid off, of course, but when something came up, he was eager to give it a try.

It was Robyn who kept him going. Fred's physician, Dr. Robert Kerlan, once remarked, "I'd say that Robyn was a very big factor in Fred's continued vitality."

In fact, one day in 1985, Robyn brought Fred to him to be treated for a fractured wrist. Kerlan was concerned. How had Fred managed to sustain a fracture of the wrist?

"I was skateboarding," Fred told him. "Slipped. That's all."

As Kerlan treated the fracture, he chatted with Fred about his active life.

"Robyn keeps me on my toes, so I've got to stay in shape," Fred confessed to him.

Was he happy in his marriage to her? Kerlan wondered.

"Everybody laughed when I got married," Fred told him. "They said it was just a May-December romance and it wouldn't last. Well, we fooled them!"

Kerlan conceded that they had done so.

"And I'll tell you, overall, it's been the best time of my life," Fred said. "Robyn has given me the reason to go on—one day at a time. We have so much in common that we can just sit and talk for hours. I'd be a lonely and miserable old man if it weren't for her."

On June 12, 1987, Robyn decided that Fred was not getting over a cold rapidly enough, and she had him admitted to Century City Hospital under the name of Fred Giles. Robyn was smart enough to know that if the press found out Fred was in the hospital, they would swarm in on him like locusts. She wanted him quiet and left in peace.

Medical tests showed that Fred had pneumonia. Three days after admission, he suddenly took a turn for the worse. He was put on a respirator to help him breathe. Robyn maintained a constant vigil at his side. She sat there for hours, holding his hand and talking to him. She told him what their friends were doing and what was in the news that was interesting and funny.

"No downbeat stuff," as she put it.

When he would break out in perspiration, she would wipe his forehead. A dozen times a day she would kiss him on the cheek and whisper, "I love you."

There was a tube in his throat; he was unable to answer her. But he would smile as if telling her, "I love you, too."

When he fell asleep, she would whisper, "Dear God, I love him so much. Don't let him leave me."

Ten days after his admission he died.

"I just put my arms around him and he died."

One member of Fred's family summed up those last years:

> Robyn and Fred were very happy over the past seven years. No one ever thought the marriage would last, but they proved everyone wrong. If it hadn't been for Robyn, Fred would never have held on as long as he did. He died a very happy man.

He died a very happy man who had made millions of other people happy during his lifetime. And for that reason, and for the fact that he was a man of integrity, of goodwill, and of compassion for others, he lived a wonderful life of his own himself.

Epilogue

"What Took Them So Long?"

It was Ginger Rogers, perhaps, who said it best:

> One thing upsets me. There's great sadness in the fact that
> Fred never won an Academy Award. It's a shame that the
> Academy of Arts and Sciences never saw fit to open their
> hearts to musical comedy. The truth is, they still haven't.
> They should have honored Fred. He was a craftsman who
> loved his work.

True, in 1949 the Motion Picture Academy of Arts and Sciences
did present him a Special Award "for his unique artistry and his
contribution to the technique of musical pictures." Ginger presented the award herself. But it was, admittedly, a pretty lame
excuse for the Academy's monumental inconsideration of the talents of this very special man.

Realizing the lack of suitable industry recognition for Fred, the
Film Society of Lincoln Center, along with the Museum of Modern
Art and the City Center of Music and Drama, cosponsored a
tribute to him at Philharmonic Hall (now Avery Fisher Hall) in
1973. It was a two-and-a-half-hour gala, for which Fred selected
40 dance excerpts from 2 hundred routines in his films. He received three standing ovations from the huge crowd that attended.
Present were four of his dance partners through his long dancing
life: his sister Adele, Ginger Rogers, Cyd Charisse, and Joan
Fontaine.

In 1978 he was honored by the Academy of Television Arts and
Sciences as the recipient of one of the first of the Kennedy Center
Honors for lifelong achievement. He also accepted the National
Artist Award of the American National Theater and Academy.

The climax of all these belated awards—by now people in the film industry were asking, "What took them so long?"—finally occurred in 1981 when he agreed to accept the prestigious Life Achievement Award given by the American Film Institute. Thus he became the ninth recipient of the award on April 10.

Hollywood outdid itself on that night. The scene of the ceremony was the glittering Beverly Hilton Hotel, just off Wilshire Boulevard. The place was mobbed, with fans, with lifelong associates, with friends he had not seen for years.

At his head table were his wife, Robyn; his daughter, Ava, and her husband; his son, Fred, and his wife; and Hermes Pan, whose association with Fred extended over a period of almost fifty years. Over two thousand people paid $300 apiece for seats to this gala.

It was exactly the kind of affair that Fred had spent a lifetime trying to avoid. And yet, fittingly, there was no one there who looked more at home in tails than Fred—who, typically, wore a shocking-pink sash around his waist!

The show itself was unforgettable. Emceed by Fred's old friend David Niven, who had flown in from Switzerland just for the occasion, the show included clips from many of his pictures that almost brought the crowd to its feet again and again.

And there were tributes—plenty of them.

James Cagney, no mean hoofer himself, asked the question that was on everyone's mind: "I want to know why they waited so long! No doubt in my mind, Fred Astaire is the greatest dancer I've ever seen in my life!"

Bob Fosse:

What always impressed me about Fred was his tremendous desire for perfection. I got a peek at him, rehearsing at M-G-M, even after he had mastered a movement, and he seemed to me to keep going over and over and over and over it again—until it became mechanical.

Mikhail Baryshnikov:

I have been invited to say something about how dancers feel about Fred Astaire. It's no secret we hate him. He gives us complexes because he's too perfect. His perfection is an absurdity; it's hard to face. . . . You remember the remark by Ile Nastase about Bjorn Bjorg: "We are playing tennis. He's playing something else." Fred Astaire, we are dancing, but you are doing something else.

Ginger Rogers (unable to be present because of commitments in New Orleans): "It certainly was fun, Fred. When they put us together, it was a blessed event. Working with you is a memory that I treasure. Love always, Ginger.''

President Ronald Reagan (not present in person but in spirit):

Nancy and I are very proud to extend our congratulations as the American Film Institute honors you with its life achievement award. There is nobody like you and while they say that every generation has its own style, your style reaches and delights us all.

Eleanor Powell (after joking about the fact that it was "Mr. Astaire" and "Miss Powell" for days before they called each other by their first names): "Mr. Astaire, I still wish we could do it just one more time. Long live the king!"
Cyd Charisse:

In the final scene of *The Band Wagon*, Adolph Green and Betty Comden wrote some wonderful words for me to say to Fred. They worked then. And I think they might be pretty good right now. "Fred, the whole company got together. We all chipped in and we bought you nothing. So we have nothing to give you but our gratitude, our admiration, and our love. The show's a hit, but we all agreed that no matter what happened to it, it was wonderful working with you. The show's going to run for a long time, and as far as I'm concerned, Fred, it's going to run forever.

Audrey Hepburn: "Enchanting, fleet-footed, unique, magical Fred. How proud I am to be among those fortunate few and also to have known the sweetness of this extraordinary man!"
Irving Berlin: "I don't know of anyone who deserves this tribute more than Fred Astaire. As a dancer, he stands alone; and as a singer, no one knows his way around a song any better than Fred. Apart from all this, I love him."
Hermes Pan:

Last summer I went to Italy to work on a film, and when I arrived in Rome, there was a big Fred Astaire festival going on. There were big posters of Fred plastered all over the city. But what impressed me most was an article in one of the leading magazines there, with a picture of Fred on the cover, and the title was "America, Che Bella Era." which means, "How beautiful America was, or used to be," and it went on to say that he personified what was the quality and the beauty of that era. And I think we owe Fred a debt of gratitude not only for his artistry but for the image that he portrays to the world of what this country really stands for.

Barrie Chase:

Fred, you say you've stopped dancing. I know that's not true. Watch you walk in this room, turn around, pick up a glass. That's the best dancing I expect to see. Dancing with Fred Astaire was tough for me. There were times, Fred, you were a monster—and I wish I could start it all over again!

George Stevens, Jr.:

Believe it or not, we are faced with a division of opinion about Fred Astaire. We say he is a genius. He says, "I'm just an old so-and-so from Omaha." I remember the words of the poet John Milton, words that could have been written for Fred Astaire: "Grace was in all his steps, heaven in his eyes, and in every gesture, dignity and love."

When Fred got up to reply, he referred to the clips that had been shown of his dance routines. "I saw things up there that I don't remember doing—and I'm glad to say I liked what I saw. I said, "My god, I didn't know that was *that* good."

Then, with disarming honesty, he looked around and seemed to be trying to explain all those seventy-five years of blood, sweat, and tears:

All the dances in the film clips shown tonight looked good to me. When you do a movie—and I know Gene Kelly will agree with me—you're sometimes alittle disappointed in what you're doing. But tonight I'm proud. I'm proud that it still hangs on!

It will hang on, Fred—forever.

Fred Astaire's Stage Musicals

Note: The following list includes the year, the show's title, Astaire's dance partner(s), composer(s) (W for words; M for music), producer, and theater of opening.

1917. *Over the Top.* Adele Astaire. (W) Charles Manning, Matthew Woodward; (M) Sigmund Romberg, Herman Timberg. Messrs. Shubert. 44th Street Roof, New York.

1918. *Passing Show of 1918.* Adele Astaire. (W) Harold Atteridge; (M) Sigmund Romberg, Jean Schwartz. Messrs. Shubert. Winter Garden, New York.

1919. *Apple Blossoms.* Adele Astaire. (W) William LeBaron; (M) Fritz Kreisler, Victor Jacobi. Charles Dillingham. Globe, New York.

1921. *The Love Letter.* Adele Astaire. (W) William LeBaron; (M) Victor Jacobi. Charles Dillingham. Globe, New York.

1922. *For Goodness Sake.* Adele Astaire. (W) Arthur Jackson; (M) William Daly, Paul Lannin. Alex A. Aarons. Lyric, New York.

1922. *The Bunch and Judy.* Adele Astaire. (W) Anne Caldwell; (M) Jerome Kern. Charles Dillingham. Globe, New York.

1923. *Stop Flirting (For Goodness Sake,* see above). Producer, Alfred Butt. Shaftsbury, London.

1924. *Lady, Be Good!* Adele Astaire. (W) Ira Gershwin; (M) George Gershwin. Alex A. Aarons, Vinton Freedley. Liberty Theater, New York.

1926. *Lady, Be Good!* (see above). Producers, Aarons, Freedley, and Alfred Butt. Empire, London.

1927. *Funny Face.* Adele Astaire. (W) Ira Gershwin; (M) George Gershwin. Alex A. Aarons, Vinton Freedley. Alvin, New York.

1928. *Funny Face* (see above). Producers, Aarons, Freedley, and Alfred Butt. Prince's, London.

1930. *Smiles.* Adele Astaire, Marilyn Miller. (W) Clifford Grey, Harold Adamson, Ring Lardner; (M) Vincent Youmans. Florenz Ziegfeld. Ziegfeld, New York.

1931. The Band Wagon. Adele Astaire, Tilly Losch. (W) Howard Dietz; (M) Arthur Schwartz). Max Gordon. New Amsterdam, New York.

1932. Gay Divorce. *Claire Luce. (WM) Cole Porter. Dwight Deere Wiman, Tom Weatherly. Ethel Barrymore, New York.*

1933. Gay Divorce (see above). Producer, Lee Ephraim. Palace, London.

Fred Astaire's Movies

Note: The following listing includes the year of release, title, Astaire's dance partner(s), composer(s) (W for words, M for music), producer, and studio. Numbers in parentheses, for example, (1)*, refer to VCR distributors named at the end of the list.

1933. *Dancing Lady.* Joan Crawford. Various. David O. Selznick. M-G-M. (4)*.
1933. *Flying Down to Rio.* Ginger Rogers, Dolores Del Rio. (W) Edward Eliscu, Gus Kahn; (M) Vincent Youmans. Louis Brock. RKO. (5)*.
1934. *The Gay Divorcée.* Ginger Rogers. Cole Porter et al. Pandro S. Berman. RKO. (5)*.
1935. *Roberta.* Ginger Rogers. (W) Otto Harbach, Dorothy Fields; (M) Jerome Kern. Pandro S. Berman. RKO. (4)*.
1935. *Top Hat.* Ginger Rogers. (WM) Irving Berlin. Pandro S. Berman. RKO. (8)*.
1936. *Follow the Fleet.* Ginger Rogers. (WM) Irving Berlin. Pandro S. Berman. RKO. (8)*.
1936. *Swing Time.* Ginger Rogers. (W) Dorothy Fields; (M) Jerome Kern. Pandro S. Berman. RKO. (8)*.
1937. *A Damsel in Distress.* George Burns, Gracie Allen. (W) Ira Gershwin; (M) George Gershwin. Pandro S. Berman. RKO. (8)*.
1937. *Shall We Dance.* Ginger Rogers. (W) Ira Gershwin; (M) George Gershwin. Pandro S. Berman. RKO. (8)*.
1938. *Carefree.* Ginger Rogers. (WM) Irving Berlin. Pandro S. Berman. RKO. (8)*.
1939. *The Story of Vernon and Irene Castle.* Ginger Rogers. Various. George Haight. RKO. (5)*.
1940. *Broadway Melody of 1940.* Eleanor Powell, George Murphy. (WM) Cole Porter. Jack Cummings. M-G-M. (4)*.
1940. *Second Chorus.* Paulette Goddard. (W) Johnny Mercer; (M) Various. Boris Morros. Paramount. (2)*.
1941. *You'll Never Get Rich.* Rita Hayworth. (WM) Cole Porter. Samuel Bischoff. Columbia. (7)*.
1942. *Holiday Inn.* Virginia Dale, Marjorie Reynolds. (WM) Irving Berlin. Mark Sandrich. Paramount. (3)*.
1942. *You Were Never Lovelier.* Rita Hayworth. (W) Johnny Mercer; (M) Jerome Kern. Louis F. Edelman. Columbia. (7)*.
1943. *The Sky's the Limit.* Joan Leslie. (W) Johnny Mercer; (M) Harold Arlen. David Hempstead. RKO. (8)*.
1945. *Yolanda and the Thief.* Lucille Bremer. (W) Arthur Freed; (M) Harry Warren. Arthur Freed. M-G-M. (4)*.
1946. *Blue Skies.* Olga San Juan. (WM) Irving Berlin. Sol C. Siegel. Paramount.
1946. *Ziegfeld Follies.* Lucille Bremer, Gene Kelly. Various. Arthur Freed. M-G-M. (4)*.
1948. *Easter Parade.* Judy Garland, Ann Miller. (WM) Irving Berlin. Arthur Freed. M-G-M. (4)*.
1949. *The Barkleys of Broadway.* Ginger Rogers. (W) Ira Gershwin; (M) George Gershwin. Arthur Freed. M-G-M.

1950. *Three Little Words*. Vera-Ellen. (W) Bert Kalmar; (M) Harry Ruby. Jack Cummings. M-G-M.

1950. *Let's Dance*. Betty Hutton. (WM) Frank Loesser. Robert Fellows. Paramount.

1951. *Royal Wedding*. Jane Powell. (W) Alan Jay Lerner; (M) Burton Lane. Arthur Freed. M-G-M. (4)*.

1952. *The Belle of New York*. Vera-Ellen. (W) Johnny Mercer; (M) Harry Warren. Arthur Freed. M-G-M.

1953. *The Band Wagon*. Cyd Charisse; Jack Buchanan. (W) Howard Dietz; (M) Arthur Schwartz. Arthur Freed. M-G-M. (4)*.

1955. *Daddy Long Legs*. Leslie Caron. (WM) Johnny Mercer. Samuel G. Engel. Twentieth Century-Fox.

1957. *Funny Face*. Audrey Hepburn. (W) Ira Gershwin, Leonard Gershe; (M) George Gershwin, Roger Edens. Roger Edens. Paramount. (6)*.

1957. *Silk Stockings*. Cyd Charisse. (WM) Cole Porter. Arthur Freed. M-G-M. (4)*.

1959. *On the Beach* (straight drama). Stanley Kramer. United Artists. (1)*.

1961. *The Pleasure of His Company* (straight drama). William Perlberg. Paramount.

1962. *The Notorious Landlady* (straight drama). Fred Kohlmar. Columbia.

1968. *Finian's Rainbow*. Solo dances. (W) E. Y. Harburg; (M) Burton Lane. Joseph Landon. Warner Brothers. (9)*.

1969. *Midas Run* (straight drama). Raymon Stross. Selmur.

1974. *That's Entertainment* (commentary). Jack Haley, Jr., Daniel Melnick. M-G-M. (4)*.

1974. *The Towering Inferno* (straight drama). Irwin Allen. Twentieth Century-Fox/Warner Brothers. (1)*.

1976. *The Amazing Dobermans* (straight drama). David Chudnow. Doberman Associates/ Golden Films.

1976. *That's Entertainment Part II* (host with Gene Kelly). Gene Kelly. Saul Chaplin, Daniel Melnick. (4)*.

1977. *Un Taxi Mauve* (straight drama). Catherine Winter, Giselle Rebillion. Sofracima/ Rizzoli Films.

1981. *Ghost Story* (straight drama). Burt Weissbourd. Universal. (3)*.

(1)*. CBS/Fox
(2)*. Kartes Video and others
(3)*. MCA Home Video
(4)*. M-G-M/UA Home Video
(5)*. Media Home Entertainment
(6)*. Paramount
(7)*. RCA/Columbia Pictures Home Video
(8)*. RKO Home Video
(9)*. Warner Home Video

Fred Astaire's TV Appearances

Note: The following listing includes date of appearance, type of performance (D for dramatic, M for music and/or dancing, T for talk), overall title of show or series (followed by title of play or segment), and the network.

April 3, 1955. (M) *The Toast of the Town.* Variety with Ed Sullivan. CBS.
December 1, 1957. (D) *General Electric Theater.* "Imp on a Cobweb Leash." CBS.
October 17, 1958. (M) *An Evening with Fred Astaire.* Special with Barrie Chase. NBC.
September 3, 1959. (D) *General Electric Theater.* "Man on a Bicycle." CBS.
November 4, 1959. (M) *Another Evening with Fred Astaire.* Special with Barrie Chase. NBC.
September 28, 1960. (M) *Astaire Time.* Special with Barrie Chase. NBC.
February 13, 1962 through December 27, 1962. (D) *Fred Astaire's Premier Theater.* Hosted by Fred Astaire. He appeared in five plays on ABC:
February 13, 1962. (D) "Mr. Easy."
July 10, 1962. (D) "Moment of Decision."
October 11, 1962. (D) "Guest in the House."
November 1, 1962. (D) "Mister Lucifer."
December 27, 1962. (D) "Blues for a Hanging."
October 2, 1964. (D) *Bob Hope's Chrysler Theater.* "Think Pretty." NBC.
November 22, 23, 29, 30, 1965. D) *Dr. Kildare.* He appeared in four continuous segments: "Fathers and Daughters," "A Gift of Love," "The Tent Dwellers," "Going Home." NBC.
January 22, 1966. *Hollywood Palace.* Variety program hosted by Fred Astaire, with Ethel Merman et al. ABC.
April 30, 1966. *Hollywood Palace.* Variety program hosted by Fred Astaire, with Barrie Chase et al. ABC.
February 7, 1968. *The Fred Astaire Show.* Special with Barrie Chase. NBC.
October 16, 1969 through March 9, 1970. *It Takes a Thief.* Played "Alistair Mundy," father of the series hero, in four episodes on ABC:
October 16, 1969. (D) "The Great Casino Caper."
November 6, 1969. (D) "Three Virgins of Rome."
December 4, 1969. (D) "The Second Time Around."
March 9, 1970. (D) "An Evening with Alistair Mundy."
November 10, 1970. (T) *The Dick Cavett Show.* ABC.
November 17, 1970. (D) *Movie of the Week.* "The Over-the-Hill Gang Rides Again." ABC.
December 13, 1970. (D) *Santa Claus Is Coming to Town.* ABC.
October 13, 1971. (T) *The Dick Cavett Show.* ABC.
September 9, 1972. (M) *Make Mine Red, White and Blue.* NBC.

Popular Songs Composed by Fred Astaire

Note: Listing includes year, title, (W) lyricist, and (M) cocomposer (if applicable), and stage production (if applicable).

1924. "You've Such a Lot." (W) Austin Melford. Sung by Phylliss Monkman and Austin Melford in *The Co-optimists* (London).
1927. "Tappin' the Time." (W) Jock Whitney, Jim Altemus. Sung by Joyce Barbour and company in *Shake Your Feet* (London).
1930. "Blue without You." (W) Mitchell Parish, Jim Altemus.
1930. "More and More." (W) Johnny Mercer; (M) Richard Myers. Sung by Odette Myrtil in *Tattle Tales* (Boston).
1935. "Not My Girl." (W) Desmond Carter.
1936. "I'll Never Let You Go." (W) Dave Dreyer, Jack Ellis.
1936. "I'm Building up to an Awful Let-Down." (W) Johnny Mercer. Sung by Binnie Hale and Jack Whiting in *Rise and Shine* (London).
1936. "Just One More Dance, Madame." (W) Dave Dreyer, Paul Francis Webster.
1940. "Just Like Taking Candy from a Baby." (W) Gladys Shelley.
1940. "Sweet Sorrow." (W) Gladys Shelley.
1944. "If Swing Goes, I Go too." (W) Fred Astaire. Sung by Fred Astaire in *Ziegfeld Follies* (film) but later cut.
1945. "Oh, My Achin' Back." (W) Willy Shore, Morey Amsterdam.
1952. "There's No Time Like the Present." (W) Walter Ruick.
1956. "Hello, Baby." (W) Moe Jaffe, Walter Ruick.
1956. "Lovely Melody." (W) Gladys Shelley.
1957. "Calypso Hooray." (W) Fred Astaire.
1959. "The Afterbeat." (W) Johnny Mercer.
1962. "Girls Like You." (W) Fred Astaire, Tommy Wolf; (M) Tommy Wolf.
1962. "You Worry Me." (W) Fred Astaire.
1962. "I Love Evreybody But You." (W) Ava Astaire; Fred Astaire.

Musical Numbers Choreographed
by Fred Astaire

Note: Before Astaire went to Hollywood, he staged four numbers in New York and London:

1923. Noel Coward and Gertrude Lawrence, "You Were Meant for Me." Noel Coward, "Sentiment." *London Calling!* Duke of York Theater. London.
1925. Marilyn Miller and the Boys, "The Wedding Knell." *Sunny.* New Amsterdam Theater, New York.
1930. Ginger Rogers and Allen Kearns, "Embraceable You." *Girl Crazy.* Alvin Theater, New York.

Recordings by Fred Astaire

Note: Listing includes LPs only, with year (if live), title, type (C for collection of previous records, FS for film soundtrack, TVS for TV soundtrack, L for live), producer if applicable, and record number. *None* of the singles from 1923 through 1962 is included by name.

1952. *The Astaire Story.* (L) (4 LPs) Norman Grantz. Clef MGC 1001, 1002, 1003, 1004. (Some numbers from this pressing appear also in Verve 2010 and Verve MGV2114. See below.)

1953. *The Bandwagon.* (FS) Narrated by Fred Astaire. MGM E3051.

1956. *Funny Face.* (FS) Verve MGV 15001.

1957. *Silk Stockings.* (FS) M-G-M E3542ST.

1959. *Now.* (L) Kapp KL 1165/KS 3949.

1960. *Three Evenings with Fred Astaire.* (TVS) Choreo A-1.

1968. *Finian's Rainbow.* (FS) Warner BS2550.

1971. *'S Wonderful, 'S Marvelous, 'S Gershwin.* (TVS) Daybreak 2009.

(C) *Lady, Be Good!* World Record Club 124/Monmouth-Evergreen 7026.

(C) *Funny Face.* World Record Club 125/Monmouth-Evergreen 7037.

(C) *The Band Wagon.* Vik 1001/English RAC Victor RD 7756/RCA International 1037.

(C) *Easter Parade.* M-G-M E3227/English M-G-M 2353 076.

(C) *Three Little Words.* M-G-M E3768ST/English M-G-M 2353 033.

(C) *Nothing Thrilled Us Half as Much.* Epic FLM 13103.

(C) *Fred Astaire.* Vocalion VL 3716.

(C) *Shoes With Wings On.* M-G-M E3413.

(C) *Mr. Top Hat.* Verve MGV 2010.

(C) *Easy to Dance With.* Verve MGV 2114.

(C) *Starring Fred Astaire.* Two-record collection Columbia SG32472.

Bibliography

Newspapers

Adams, Cindy. "Ginger: 'He Was a Perfectionist.' " *New York Post,* June 23, 1987.
Anderson, Jack. "Critic's Notebook; Fred Astaire's Dances Seen Frame by Frame." *New York Times,* January 30, 1986.
Arnold, Gary. "Astaire! Astaire! One Top Hat Puts on the Ritz at AFI's Fred Astaire Film Festival." *Washington Post,* March 1, 1981.
————. "Fred Astaire-Ginger Rogers Retrospective." *Washington Post,* April 27, 1977.
Barnes, Bart. "Fred Astaire Dies; Superstar Dancer." *Washington Post,* June 23, 1987.
Barnes, Clive. "Top Hat, White Tie and Tails." *New York Post,* June 23, 1987.
Bernard, Jami. "Hat's Entertainment, Fred." *New York Post,* June 23, 1987.
"Blue Skies" (rev). *Film Daily,* September 26, 1946.
"Broadway Melody of 1940" (rev). *Film Daily,* February 14, 1940.
Brooke, Jill. "Astaire Dances One More Time." *New York Post.* June 23, 1987.
Canby, Vincent. "Astaire Persona: Urbanity and Grace." *New York Times.* June 23, 1987.
"Carefree" (rev). *Film Daily,* August 30, 1938.
Cech, John. "A Fred Astaire Frog" (rev). *Christian Science Monitor,* August 23, 1985.
Cohen, Richard. "Fred Astaire: The Idol of a Kind Who Can't Dance." *Washington Post,* May 13, 1979.
Crisp, Clement. "Obituary: Fred Astaire." *Financial Times,* June 23, 1987.
"A Damsel in Distress (rev). *Film Daily,* November 20, 1937.
"Dancing Lady" (rev.) *Film Daily,* December 2, 1933.
"Fred Astaire" (editorial opinion). *Washington Post,* June 24, 1987.
"Fred Astaire, the Dazzling Dancer." *Christian Science Monitor,* June 23, 1987.
"Fred Astaire on Video." *New York Times,* July 5, 1987.
"Fred Astaire to Receive AFI Achievement Prize." *Washington Post,* November 4, 1980.
Ebert, Roger. "Style Was the Man." *New York Post,* June 23, 1987.
"Flying Down to Rio" (rev). *Film Daily,* December 20, 1933.
"Follow the Fleet" (rev). *Film Daily,* February 19, 1936.
"The Gay Divorcée" (rev). *Film Daily,* October 3, 1934.
Goldner, Nancy. "Canada's Bouquet to Fred Astaire." *Christian Science Monitor,* June 6, 1983.
Goodman, Ellen. "Top Hat, White Tie, and Sweat." *Stamford Advocate,* June 27, 1987.
"Greatest Dancer in the World: Fred Astaire Dead at 88." Associated Press, June 23, 1987.
"Holiday Inn" (rev). *Film Daily,* June 15, 1942.
Jones, Jack. "Fred Astaire, Hollywood's Greatest Dancer, Dies at 88; Succumbed in My Arms, Wife Says." *los Angeles Times,* June 22, 1987.
————. "Master of Style, Elegance Was 88; Fred Astaire, Movie's Greatest Dancer, Dies." *Los Angeles Times,* June 23, 1987.

Kart, Laurence (letter). "Astaire's Achievements." *New York Times,* July 19, 1987.

Kimmel, Daniel M. (rev). "An Admiring Look at Fred Astaire." *Christian Science Monitor,* April 2, 1985.

Kisselgoff, Anna. "Fred Astaire Perfected a New Art Form." *New York Times,* June 28, 1987.

———. "Home Video: New Cassettes from Fred Astaire to Charlie Brown." *New York Times,* July 22, 1984.

Rabinowitz, Dorothy. "Love's Not Dead, It's Only Sleeping." *New York Post,* June 26, 1987.

"The Range of Fred Astaire" (editorial). *Stamford Advocate,* June 26, 1987.

"Roberta" (rev). *Film Daily,* February 12, 1987.

Royko, Mike. "When Fred Astaire Danced into My life." *New York Daily News,* June 25, 1987.

Russell, Don. "An Evening on the Air with Astaire." *Stamford Advocate,* June 26, 1987.

Schuchat, Berthe (letter). "Fred Astaire on the Stairway to Paradise" *New York Post,* July 5, 1987.

Segal, Lewis. "Fred Astaire: A Grace Period Is Over." *Los Angeles Times,* June 23, 1987.

Shales, Tom. "Fred Astaire Danced Where Angels Feared to Tread." *Washington Post,* June 25, 1987.

Shepard, Richard F. "Fred Astaire, the Ultimate Dancer, Dies." *New York Times,* June 23, 1987.

Silverman, Steven M. "Astaire-Way to Heaven." *New York Post,* June 23, 1987.

———. "Stars, Stripes and Fred Astaire." *New York Post,* June 23, 1987.

Silverman, Stephen M., and Jack Schermerhorn. "Fred Astaire: He Was the Best." *New York Post,* June 23, 1987.

"The Story of Vernon and Irene Castle" (rev). *Film Daily,* March 31, 1939.

Suzy. "Track Honor for Astaire." *New York Post,* June 30, 1987.

"Swing Time" (rev). *Film Daily,* August 26, 1936.

Tallmer, Jerry. "A Dance Is a Dance . . . and More." *New York Post,* June 23, 1987.

Terry, Carol Burton. "TV Line." *Stamford Advocate,* July 14, 1987.

"Top Hat" (rev). *Film Daily,* August 16, 1935.

Turan, Kenneth. "A Tribute to Fred Astaire: A Dancer's Dancer." *Washington Post,* April 13, 1981.

"When Fred Astaire Leaves the Room." *New York Times,* June 23, 1987.

"Yolanda and the Thief" (rev.) *Film Daily,* October 19, 1945.

"You Were Never Lovelier" (rev). *Film Daily,* October 5, 1942.

"Ziegfeld Follies" (rev). *Film Daily,* January 11, 1946.

Periodicals

"Alan Jay Lerner Applauds 'A Renaissance in Theater.' " *US News & World Report,* November 26, 1979.

Albrecht, Donald (rev). "Designing Dreams." *People,* February 16, 1987.

Astaire, Fred. "Follow the Fleet." *American Magazine,* June 1936.

———. "On the Cuff." *Seventeen,* October 1966.

———. "Steps in Time." *McCall's,* April 1959.

———. "This Is the Way to Teach Your Child to Dance." *Parents Magazine,* August 1948.

"Astaire in Air." *Life,* March, 26, 1951.

"The Barkleys of Broadway" (rev). *Motion Picture Herald,* April 16, 1949.

Barnett, Lincoln. "Fred Astaire: He Is the No. 1 Exponent of America's Only Native and Original Dance Form." *Life,* August 25, 1941.

Burnet, Dana. "Watching His Step." *Pictorial Review,* January 1936.

"Carefree" (rev). *Motion Picture Herald,* September 3, 1938.

Clarke, Gerald. "The All-American Love Goddess: Rita Hayworth: 1918–1987." *Time,* May 25, 1987.

Cocks, Jay; rpt by Mitch Gelman (N.Y.) and others. "Black Tie Still Required; the Tuxedo Celebrates Its 100th Birthday, Alas." *Time,* October 29, 1986.

Conrad, Derek. "Two Feet in the Air." *Films & Filming,* December 1959.

Corliss, Richard. "Lyrics by 'The Other One'; Ira Gershwin: 1896–1983." *Time,* August 29, 1983.

"Dancing with Astaire and Rogers." *Literary Digest,* December 12, 1936.

"Dancing Feat" (rev). *Time,* March 17, 1947.

"Dancing Lady" (rev). *Literary Digest,* December 16, 1933.

"Dancing Lady" (rev). *Motion Picture Herald,* November 25, 1933.

Darrach, Brad. "He Made Us Feel Like Dancing." *People,* July 6, 1987.

Dash. "The Astaires: New Acts." *Variety,* October 17, 1908.

Davidson, Bill. "Fred Astaire: Just Beginning to Live." *Look,* November 10, 1959.

———. "Fred Astaire: The Five Women in His Life." *Look,* November 24, 1959.

"Delightful Witchery." *Newsweek,* April 1, 1957.

"Died" (Adele Astaire). *Newsweek,* February 9, 1981.

——— (Phyllis Astaire). *Newsweek,* September 27, 1954.

——— (Eleanor Powell). *Newsweek,* February 22, 1982.

——— (George Stevens). *Newsweek,* March 17, 1975.

——— (Vera-Ellen). *Newsweek,* September 14, 1981.

"Easter Parade" (rev). *Motion Picture Herald,* May 29, 1948.

Eustis, Morton. "Fred Astaire: The Actor-Dancer Attacks His Part." *Theatre Arts,* November 1941.

"Famous Pair's New Partners." *Life,* October 20, 1958.

"Fearless Fred on a Fire Escape." *Life,* August 10, 1953.

"Forty Years a Hoofer." *New York Times Magazine,* September 8, 1946.

Francke, Linda Bird. "The Happy Hoofer." *Newsweek,* April 7, 1975.

"Fred Astaire and . . ." *New York Times Magazine,* March 12, 1950.

"Fred Astaire: The One and Only; a Fact Dossier on His Career." *Vogue,* February 1, 1959.

"Fred Astaire Plots Out New Routines at His In-Laws' Home in Aiken, South Carolina." *Life,* December 30, 1940.

"Fred Astaire: Portrait." *Theatre Arts,* September 1940.

"Fred Astaire: Profile." *Dance Magazine* ("1959 Award Winners"), March 1960.

"Fred Astaire's Dancing." *Theatre Arts,* June 1936.

"Fred Astaire Succumbs at 88; World's Greatest Pop Dancer." *Variety,* June 24, 1987.

"Flying Down to Rio" (rev). *Motion Picture Herald,* December 16, 1933.

"Follow the Fleet" (rev). *Motion Picture Herald,* February 22, 1936.

"The Gay Divorcée" (rev). *Literary Digest,* December 1, 1934.

"The Gay Divorcée" (rev). *Motion Picture Herald,* October 13, 1934.

"Ginger and Old Dad." *Newsweek,* April 1, 1957.

Hall, Leonard. "That Cute Astaire." *Delineator,* December 1935.

Hutchins, David. "Leslie Caron Gets Back on Her Toes for a Role Tuto Good to Pass Up." *People,* May 14, 1984.

Jamison, Barbara Berch. "The Ageless Astaire." *New York Times Magazine,* August 2, 1953.

Jarvis, John. "The Brother and Sister Who Never Quarrel." *American Magazine,* December 1931.

Khan, Princess Jasmin Aga. "Remembering Rita." *Time,* June 1, 1987.

Knight, Arthur. "Choreography for Camera." *Dance Magazine,* May 1957.

———. "Hommage à Fred Astaire." *Saturday Review,* July 25, 1953.

Kroll, Jack. "A Buck, a Wing and a Smile." *Newsweek,* January 9, 1984.

———. "The Joy of Dancin'." *Newsweek,* April 10, 1978.

———. "Never Gonna Dance Again." *Newsweek,* July 6, 1987.

Landers, Robert K. "The Tux Is Born." *Congressional Quarterly,* October 2, 1986.

Leamy, Hugh. "The Ascending Astaires." *Collier's,* March 31, 1928.

Lerman, Les. "Point of Departure." *Mademoiselle,* September 1959.

"Looking at the Star," *Newsweek,* April 1, 1957.

"Married" (Fred Astaire and Robyn Smith). *Newsweek,* July 7, 1980.

McGuigan, Cathleen. "Newsmakers." *Newsweek*, March 17, 1980, April 6, 1981.
McLaughlin. "Something in the Way He Moved." & World *Report*, July 6, 1987.
"Merian C. Cooper." *Films in Review*, January 1966.
"Milestones" (Adele Astaire). *Time*, February 9, 1981.
———— (Fred Astaire). *Time*, July 6, 1987.
———— (Vera-Ellen). *Time*, September 14, 1981.
Morrow, Lance. "In Praise of Serious Hats." *Time*, April 25, 1983.
Nichols, M. "Ageless Astaire." *Coronet*, May 1957.
Novak, Ralph. "Ginger and Fred." *People*, April 14, 1980.
————. "That's Dancing." *People*, February 4, 1985.
"One of the Finest Hours." *Newsweek*, October 27, 1958.
"On Tuxes and Bad Taste." *Newsweek*, October 6, 1986.
O'Toole, Lawrence. "Saving the Last Dance; Ginger and Fred." *Maclean's*, April 14, 1986.
"Picks and Pans, Screen" *(Ghost Story)*. *People*, January 11, 1982.
RC. "Can Dance a Little." *Time*, November 16, 1981.
"Roberta" (rev). *Literary Digest*, March 23, 1935.
"Roberta" (rev). *Motion Picture Herald*, February 23, 1935.
Roeder, Bill. "Newsmakers." *Newsweek*, May 24, 1976.
"Shall We Dance" (rev). *Motion Picture Herald*, May 8, 1937.
Shapiro, Laura. "An Early Peek into Santa's Bag." *Newsweek*, December 9, 1985.
Shipp, Cameron. "How to Dance Like Four Antelopes." *Collier's*, January 8, 1949.
Simon, B. "Fred Astaire—Slow and Intimate." *Saturday Review*, February 28, 1953.
Smith, Robert G. "How Fred Astaire Found Joy in His Final Years with a Wife Half His Age." *National Enquirer*, July 7, 1987.
"Still Packing Them in After All These Years." *US News & World Report*, May 5, 1986.
"The Story of Vernon and Irene Castle" (rev). *Motion Picture Herald*, April 1, 1939.
"The Story of Vernon and Irene Castle" (rev). *Stage*, April 1, 1939.
Swan, Annalyn. "Old Hoofers Never Die." *Newsweek*, April 28, 1980.
"Swing Time" (rev). *Motion Picture Herald*, August 29, 1936.
"Swing Time" (rev). *Stage*, October 1936.
Swisher, Viola Hegyi. "A Special for the Special: Fred Astaire and Partner Barrie Chase." *Dance Magazine*, June 1968.
Terry, Walker. "World of Dance." *Saturday Review*, March 1, 1969.
Thomas, Bob. "Astaire: The Man, the Dancer." *People*, December 3, 1984.
"Top Hat" (rev). *Literary Digest*, September 7, 1935.
"Triple Trouble." *Collier's*, July 25, 1953.
Zetlin, D., ed. "Old Dog's New Tricks at 66: Interview." *Life*, October 29, 1965.

Books

Albrecht, Donald. *Designing Dreams: Modern Architecture in the Movies*. New York: Harper & Row, 1986.
Astaire, Fred. *Steps in Time*. New York: Harper & Brothers, 1959.
Atkinson, Brooks. *Broadway*. New York: The Macmillan Co., 1970.
Blum, Daniel. *A Pictorial History of the Silent Screen*. New York: G. P. Putnam's Sons, 1953.
Croce, Arlene. *The Fred Astaire and Ginger Rogers Book*. New York: Outerbridge & Lazard, Inc., 1972.
Green, Abel and Joe Laurie, Jr. *Show Biz: From Vaude to Video*. New York: Henry Holt & Co., 1951.
Green, Stanley. *The World of Musical Comedy*. New York: Ziff-Davis Publishing Co., 1960.
Green, Stanley, and Burt Godlblatt. *Starring Fred Astaire*. New York: Dodd, Mead & Co., 1973.

Halliwell, Leslie. *The Filmgoer's Companion*. New York: Equinox Books, 1965, 1967, 1970.

Hirschhorn, Clive. *The Hollywood Musical*. New York: Crown Publishers, Inc., 1981.

Laurie, Joe, Jr. *Vaudeville: From the Honky-Tonks to the Palace*. New York: Henry Holt & Co., 1953.

Michael, Paul. *The Academy Awards: A Pictorial History*. New York: Crown Publishing, Inc., 1982.

Moody, Richard. *Dramas from the American Theatre: 1762– 1909*. Cleveland, New York: World Publishing Co., 1966.

Mueller, John. *Astaire Dancing: The Musical Films*. New York: Alfred A. Knopf, 1985.

Niven, David. *Bring on the Empty Horses*. New York: G. P. Putnam's Sons, 1975.

Pickard, Roy. *Fred Astaire*. New York: Crescent Books, 1985.

Thomas, Bob. *Astaire: The Man, the Dancer*. New York: St. Martin's Press, 1984.

Zierold, Norman. *The Monguls*. New York: Avon Books, 1969.